1,000 AMAZING DINOSAUR FACTS

DK | Penguin Random House

Senior editor Shaila Brown
Project art editor Joe Lawrence
Designers Sunita Gahir, Peter Radcliffe, Samantha Richiardi
Senior picture researcher Aditya Katyal
Illustrators Adam Benton, Peter Bull, Stuart Jackson-Carter, Arran Lewis, Naomi Murray, Gus Scott
Creative retouching Adam Brackenbury, Steve Crozier
Managing editor Rachel Fox
Managing art editor Owen Peyton Jones
Production editor Gillian Reid
Senior production controller Meskerem Berhane
Jacket designer Stephanie Cheng Hui Tan
Senior jackets coordinator Priyanka Sharma Saddi
Jacket design development manager Sophia MTT
Publisher Andrew Macintyre
Associate publishing director Liz Wheeler
Art director Karen Self
Publishing director Jonathan Metcalf

Authors
Stevie Derrick, Dean Lomax,
John Woodward

Consultant
Professor Paul Barrett

First published in Great Britain in 2023
by Dorling Kindersley Limited
DK, One Embassy Gardens, 8 Viaduct Gardens,
London, SW11 7BW

The authorised representative in the EEA is
Dorling Kindersley Verlag GmbH. Arnulfstr. 124,
80636 Munich, Germany

Copyright © 2023 Dorling Kindersley Limited
A Penguin Random House Company
10 9 8 7 6 5 4 3 2 1
001–331888–August/2023

A CIP catalogue record for this book is available
from the British Library.

ISBN: 978-0-2415-6993-1

Printed and bound in China

For the curious
www.dk.com

MIX
Paper | Supporting
responsible forestry
FSC™ C018179

This book was made with Forest
Stewardship Council™ certified
paper – one small step in DK's
commitment to a sustainable future.
For more information go to
www.dk.com/our-green-pledge

1,000 AMAZING DINOSAUR FACTS

CONTENTS

1 AGE OF GIANTS

2 DINOSAUR BIOLOGY

3 CURIOUS CREATURES

4 FANTASTIC FOSSILS

5 DINOSAUR WORLD

Age of giants

For at least 135 million years, during the Mesozoic Era, life on planet Earth was dominated by the biggest, heaviest, most spectacular and terrifying land animals the world has ever seen – the giant dinosaurs.

The earliest known dinosaurs lived in the Triassic Period, but the real giants evolved in the Jurassic. In what is now North America, they included fearsome predators like *Allosaurus*, seen here attacking a colossal *Brontosaurus*.

WHEN DID
DINOSAURS
EXIST?

Dinosaurs ruled the world during the Mesozoic Era, an immense stretch of time that is divided into three periods. They first appeared during the Triassic Period and rose to dominance in the Jurassic before most of them became extinct at the end of the Cretaceous Period. Today, the sole surviving group of dinosaurs are the birds, which are found on every continent on Earth.

FAST FACTS

In 1842, palaeontologist Richard Owen realized that the fossils of *Iguanodon*, *Megalosaurus*, and *Hylaeosaurus* belonged to a group of extinct animals. He called this new group dinosaurs, meaning "terrible lizards".

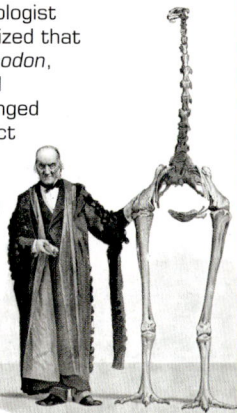

Richard Owen with a skeleton of an extinct moa

This plant-eating dinosaur was one of the longest dinosaurs that ever lived.

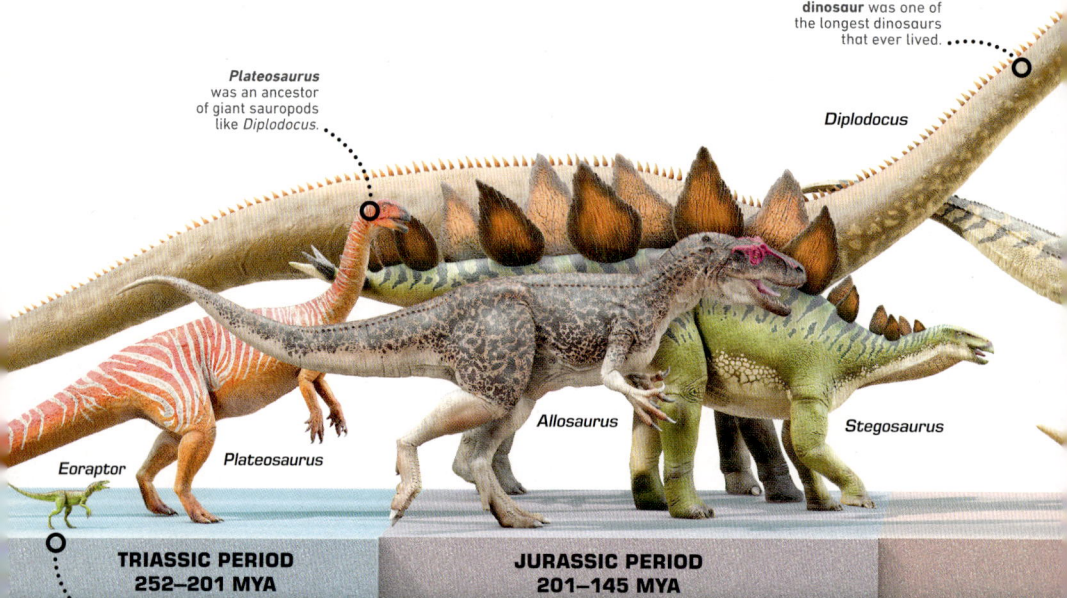

Plateosaurus was an ancestor of giant sauropods like *Diplodocus*.

Diplodocus

Allosaurus

Stegosaurus

Eoraptor

Plateosaurus

**TRIASSIC PERIOD
252–201 MYA**

**JURASSIC PERIOD
201–145 MYA**

Eoraptor was about the size of a fox.

MESOZOIC ERA

SCIENTISTS ESTIMATE THAT 65% OF DINOSAURS WERE **PLANT-EATERS**.

THE FIRST **BIRD-LIKE** DINOSAURS EVOLVED DURING THE JURASSIC PERIOD.

The first dinosaurs appeared during the Triassic Period.

Dinosaurs existed on Earth for more than 235 million years. By comparison, modern humans have existed for only 300,000 years. Our species, called *Homo sapiens*, is the last surviving member of *Homo*, which evolved in Africa almost 3 MYA.

DINOSAUR EVOLUTION

No dinosaur species lived throughout the whole of the Mesozoic Era. For example, dinosaurs living in the Triassic and Jurassic periods would be fossils under the feet of dinosaurs in the Cretaceous Period. In fact, many ancient animals evolved and become extinct long before the dinosaurs first appeared.

Deinonychus
115–110 MYA

Brachiosaurus
155–145 MYA

Coelophysis
216–200 MYA

Dimetrodon
295–272 MYA

A ferocious predator, *Tyrannosaurus* hunted plant-eaters such as the massive *Triceratops*.

Tyrannosaurus

Uintatherium was a rhino-sized mammal.

QUATERNARY 2.5 MYA TO PRESENT

Homo habilis

Dryopithecus

Triceratops

Uintatherium

CRETACEOUS PERIOD 145–66 MYA

PALEOGENE 66–23 MYA

NEOGENE 23–2.5 MYA

CENOZOIC ERA

99.9 99.9% OF ALL SPECIES THAT HAVE EVER EXISTED ARE NOW EXTINCT.

TYRANNOSAURUS LIVED CLOSER IN TIME TO HUMANS THAN IT DID TO STEGOSAURUS.

WHAT WAS THE
HEAVIEST
DINOSAUR?

Titanosaurs were a group of sauropod dinosaurs that included the largest land animals to have ever lived. And *Argentinosaurus* is thought to be the largest of them all. From just a few fragments of fossils, including a couple of ribs, some bones from the spine, and two leg bones, scientists have worked out this dinosaur's colossal size. Stomping through forests during the Late Cretaceous period, *Argentinosaurus* spent its whole life devouring any plant in its path.

The incredibly long neck enabled *Argentinosaurus* to feed from the treetops.

The long muscular tail was used for balance and for lashing out at predators.

FAST FACTS

This massive *Argentinosaurus* fibula bone (lower leg bone) is 155 cm (61 in) long — about the same as the height of an average 12-year-old. It was discovered in 1987 on a farm in Argentina.

Many titanosaurs had stump-like hand bones, called metacarpals, which formed a vertical weight-bearing column. These are the same bones that form the palm of your hands.

FEMALES LAID UP TO **40 EGGS** AT A TIME AND THESE WERE THE SIZE OF A **SMALL MELON**.

40 AN *ARGENTINOSAURUS* BABY MAY HAVE TAKEN **40 YEARS** TO GROW FROM 5 KG (11 LB) TO 75 TONNES (83 TONS).

SOUTH AMERICAN GIANT

Argentinosaurus gets its name from the country where its fossils were first discovered — modern-day Argentina. However, the landscape of Argentina looked very different then. Covered in lush forests and sweeping plains, the prehistoric continent of South America was home to a huge variety of gigantic sauropods.

Fossil sites in South America suggest that *Argentinosaurus* lived in an arid habitat.

Weighing an incredible 75 tonnes (83 tons) – about the same weight as 38 family cars – everything about this dinosaur was supersized. It was strongly built with massive bones and muscles, which supported its immense weight. The largest of the bones discovered so far is a vertebra (backbone), which is 1.6 m (5 ft) tall and 1.2 m (4 ft) wide.

Argentinosaurus may have been the **heaviest** animal to have ever walked on Earth.

ARGENTINOSAURUS MUNCHED UP TO 230 KG (500 LB) OF **PLANT FOOD** EVERY DAY.

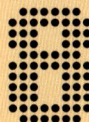

ARGENTINOSAURUS PLODDED ALONG AT A **TOP SPEED** OF 8 KPH (5 MPH).

LEAF-EATING GIANTS

The fossilized footprints of plant-eating dinosaurs show that they travelled in herds, often with young ones protected by the bigger adults — just like elephants today. Giant sauropods like these colossal *Alamosaurus* may have had to roam over vast areas to find enough food to satisfy their huge appetites. Their very long necks enabled them to gather leaves from high in the treetops, and they could reach even higher by rearing up on their hind legs.

Sauropod fossils have been found throughout the world except Antarctica.

WHAT WAS THE LARGEST
CARNIVOROUS
DINOSAUR?

Excavated from the deserts of North Africa, the 100-million-year-old bones of *Spinosaurus* show that it could have been the biggest hunter that ever lived – even bigger than the mighty *Tyrannosaurus*. Since no complete skeleton has been found we may never be sure, but some scientists think it could have been up to 18 m (59 ft) long, which is longer than a school bus.

Spinosaurus was the largest meat-eating dinosaur.

FAST FACTS

Small pores in the snout could have contained water pressure sensors to help detect invisible prey in murky water.

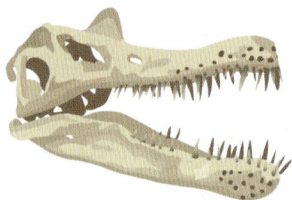

Three-fingered hands and curved claws may have been used to seize fish. They could hold onto prey ready for the hunter's snapping jaws.

Long pointed teeth were ideal for catching slippery prey.

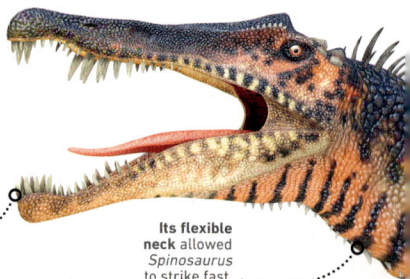

Its flexible neck allowed *Spinosaurus* to strike fast.

THE ORIGINAL *SPINOSAURUS* FOSSILS WERE DESTROYED DURING WORLD WAR II.

SPINOSAURUS'S SKULL AND TEETH WERE LIKE THOSE OF A MODERN CROCODILE.

SAIL OR HUMP?

The strangest features of this dinosaur are the long spines projecting from its backbone. As tall as an adult human, they may have formed a flat "sail" that helped it lose heat by acting like a radiator. But they could also have supported a hump like that of a camel or been used to attract mates.

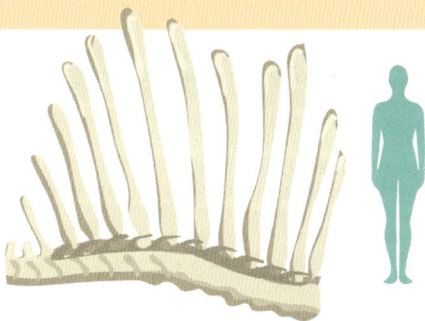

The huge sail added to *Spinosaurus*'s menacing size.

The fossil remains of *Spinosaurus* have always puzzled scientists. There is no doubt that it was very big, but it seems to have been a strange shape, with unusually short hind legs, a deep, paddle-like tail, and a tall sail-like feature on its back. How these adaptations helped it thrive in its swampy habitat is still debated. However, its colossal size and crocodile-like jaws, lined with long, pointed teeth, made it a formidable hunter.

SPINOSAURUS PROBABLY HAD A **HALF-AQUATIC LIFESTYLE**, PREYING ON BIG FISH AS WELL AS SEIZING OTHER DINOSAURS.

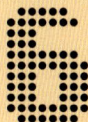

6 THE NUMBER OF FRAGMENTARY *SPINOSAURUS* SPECIMENS FOUND SO FAR.

Spinosaurus's **tooth-studded jaw** was about 1 m (3 ft) long.

FISH HUNTER

We know from chemical analysis of its teeth that *Spinosaurus* ate a lot of fish (such as this prehistoric sawfish), but did it hunt them underwater like a crocodile? Its powerful tail seems ideally shaped to drive it through the water, and its tall sail may have helped keep it stable as it swept its jaws sideways to snatch a victim. But evidence from a related dinosaur called *Baryonyx* suggests that *Spinosaurus* also attacked land animals, possibly when they visited the water to drink.

Supersaurus was longer than a tennis court and weighed as much as 40 tonnes (44 tons). With a head the size of a horse and hips as wide as a car, it was also among the world's largest dinosaurs.

The whip-like tail was used as a counterbalance to its long neck.

A tennis court is 24 m (78 ft) long.

WHAT WAS THE
LONGEST
DINOSAUR?

Belonging to the diplodocid family – a group of long-necked dinosaurs – *Supersaurus* was a massive plant-eater that roamed the swampy marshlands of the Late Jurassic period, around 150 MYA. It measured 39 m (128 ft) from snout to tail, and had one of the longest sauropod necks in relation to its body length. Scientists know of this dinosaur's humongous size from just a few fossils, including some bones from its spine.

4 THE **FASTEST HUMAN** WOULD HAVE TAKEN 4 SECONDS TO RUN THE LENGTH OF *SUPERSAURUS*.

THE **TIP OF ITS TAIL** COULD MOVE FASTER THAN THE SPEED OF SOUND – AROUND 1,234 KPH (767 MPH).

It is thought that *Supersaurus* walked with its neck parallel to the ground, rather than standing upright.

WORLD'S LONGEST ANIMAL

While *Supersaurus* was the longest dinosaur, it isn't the longest animal. At 46 m (151 ft) in length — about the same as five buses — a deep-sea animal called a siphonophore holds that record. A siphonophore is actually a collection of tiny animals that cannot live on their own. Each member has a different task, for example, some catch prey while others digest food.

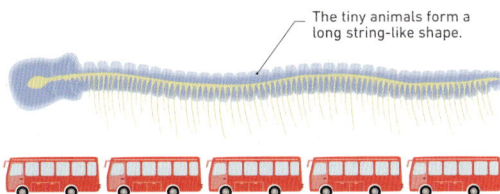

The tiny animals form a long string-like shape.

Supersaurus may have been the **longest** dinosaur to have ever walked on land.

SUPERSAURUS'S **NECK** REACHED A WHOPPING 15 M (50 FT) IN LENGTH.

A DINOSAUR SKELETON NAMED **JIMBO** IS THE MOST COMPLETE *SUPERSAURUS* EVER DISCOVERED.

FAST FACTS

With a height of up to 6 m (20 ft), the giraffe is the tallest living animal. It has seven neck bones — the same number as humans but each neck bone is extra long.

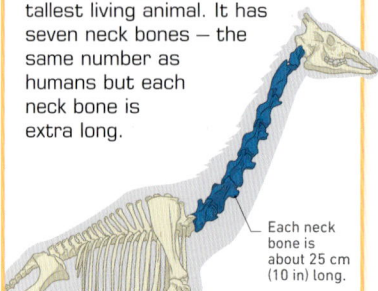

Each neck bone is about 25 cm (10 in) long.

The ostrich has the longest neck of any bird. Unlike a giraffe, it uses it to reach down to feed on plants and tiny animals.

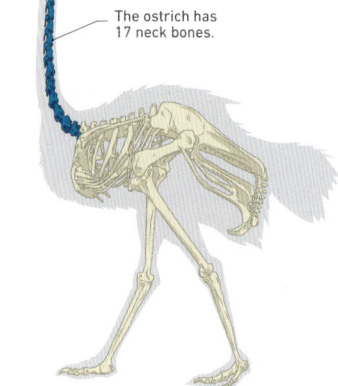

The ostrich has 17 neck bones.

HOW HIGH COULD A
DINOSAUR REACH?

Sauropods had the longest necks of any known animal and although a complete set of neck bones haven't been found, scientists estimate that *Sauroposeidon*'s neck would have been the longest. It is known from only four enormous neck bones — the longest measured 1.25 m (4 ft) and based on this, its tiny head may have stretched 18 m (60 ft) off the ground.

Sauroposeidon **may have been able to reach as high as a** six-storey building.

Like most sauropods, the tail was extremely long and used for balance.

***Sauroposeidon* roamed** central North America, about 110 MYA. With its supersized neck, it could extend much higher when feeding from the treetops without having to rear up. Compared to a brachiosaur, with a 9-m (30-ft) long neck, *Sauroposeidon* could reach over twice as much food.

SAUROPOSEIDON'S NECK BONES WERE FIRST FOUND IN OKLAHOMA, USA, IN 1994.

THE LARGEST BLOCK OF ROCK CONTAINING *SAUROPOSEIDON'S* NECK BONES WEIGHED 3 TONNES (3.3 TONS).

In relation to its body size, *Sauroposeidon* had one of the smallest heads of any animal.

Like other sauropods, *Sauroposeidon*'s bones had air-filled cavities, making the bones incredibly light. They were also very thin-walled — in some places the bone was no thicker than an eggshell.

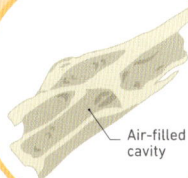

Air-filled cavity

SPIKED-NECKED DINOSAUR

Bajadasaurus, a sauropod that lived about 145 MYA in Patagonia, Argentina, had a very unusual neck. As well as being long, it had curved spikes jutting out of its neck. The spikes were paired and may have sported a sail of skin on each side.

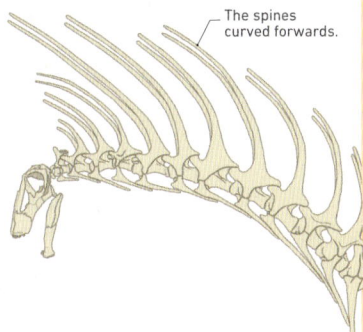

The spines curved forwards.

AT 13 M (43 FT), THE ASIAN SAUROPOD *XINJIANGTITAN* HAS THE LONGEST COMPLETE SET OF NECK BONES.

***SAUROPOSEIDON* MEANS "EARTHQUAKE GOD LIZARD" IN GREEK.**

DID DINOSAURS HAVE
FEATHERS?

Scientists used to think that all dinosaurs had scaly skin, like modern reptiles. Some certainly did, especially the very big ones. But in the 1990s the discovery of superbly preserved fossils in Liaoning, China, revealed that many small theropods – the mainly meat-eating dinosaurs that walked on two legs – had feathers. Some were very simple feathers that would have looked like fuzz, but others resembled those of modern birds.

Long plumes
The arm bones of the eagle-sized hunter *Velociraptor* had small knobs that would have anchored long, broad-vaned feathers. Since they were not big enough for flight they were probably mainly for show, but we also know that similar dinosaurs used them to brood their eggs and young.

Velociraptor's **body** would have been covered with feathers.

Sciurumimus had a long fluffy tail, which helped it balance.

Fuzzy pelt
Fossils of the tiny, squirrel-like *Sciurumimus* reveal that its body was covered with fuzz-like filaments known as protofeathers. These would have provided insulation, like fur, to stop it losing vital body heat.

THE **FIRST FOSSIL DINOSAUR FEATHER** WAS DISCOVERED IN 1860, IN ROCKS THAT ARE 150 MILLION YEARS OLD.

SIMPLE FEATHERS MAY HAVE EVOLVED MORE THAN 80 MILLION YEARS BEFORE THE EARLIEST BIRD TOOK TO THE AIR.

HOW FEATHERS EVOLVED

Feathers seem to have evolved from simple strand-like structures that kept small dinosaurs warm. Over time they became more complex, with branching barbs. These eventually gained tiny hooks that zipped them together into vanes, permitting flight.

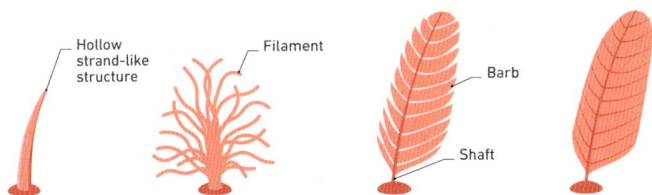

Hollow strand-like structure

Filament

Barb

Shaft

Protofeathers
The earliest feathers were hollow, flexible strands.

Fluffy down
Extra filaments made feathers fluffier and more effective as insulation.

Fluff to feather
Rows of barbs sprouting from a shaft formed the basic feather shape.

Final touch
Hooks formed on the barbs, linking them to create flight feathers.

Taking off
Some close relatives of *Velociraptor* had much longer, well-feathered forelimbs. They were too long to be just for show, so it is likely that these dinosaurs could fly. But the most famous, *Archaeopteryx*, probably could not fly for long because it did not have big wing muscles like a modern bird.

The tail was a fan of feathers, like the tail of a modern bird.

The wings had fully developed flight feathers.

Airborne
Towards the end of the Mesozoic age of dinosaurs, the skies were full of flying creatures similar to modern birds. Some, including the gull-like *Ichthyornis*, still had teeth, but they had lost their long bony tails. Their powerful wing muscles enabled them to fly well.

ICHTHYORNIS MEANS "FISH BIRD" BECAUSE IT MAY HAVE USED ITS LONG, TOOTHED JAWS TO CATCH SLIPPERY FISH.

SO FAR, ALMOST ALL FOSSIL DINOSAURS FOUND WITH FEATHERS HAVE BEEN THEROPODS – THE GROUP THAT INCLUDES BIRDS.

FEATHERED FOSSIL

Found in Germany in 1874, this fossil is one of several specimens of *Archaeopteryx*, which is often described as the first known bird. There are traces of feathers visible in the rock, but it also had features similar to the small theropod dinosaurs of its time, including teeth and a long, bony tail. Scientists had assumed it was different from them because of its feathers, but the fossils found in China in the 1990s showed that many small theropod dinosaurs had feathers too. However, unlike them, *Archaeopteryx* had wings that seem too long to be useful for anything but flight.

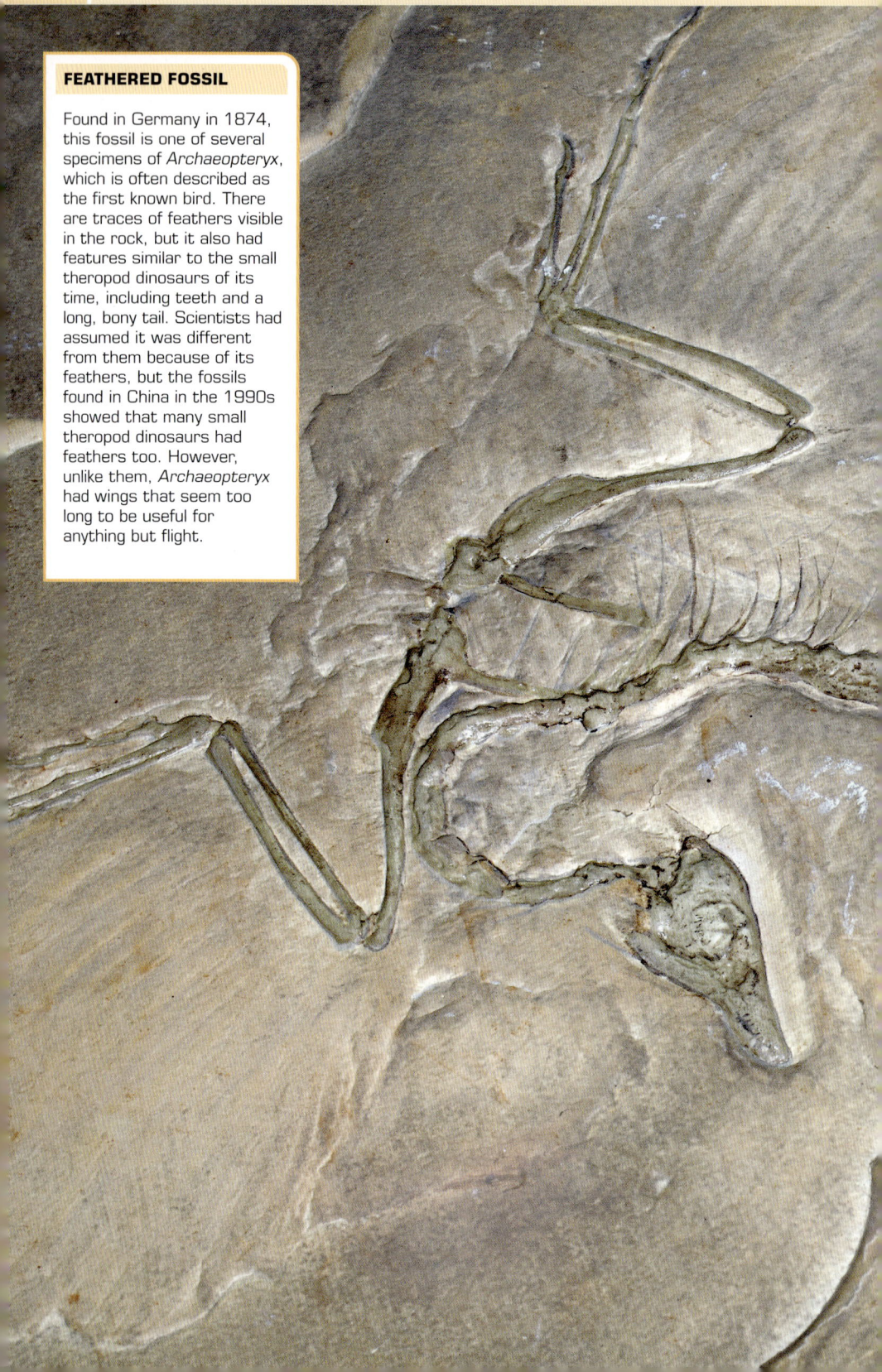

This *Archaeopteryx* fossil shows that there is a link between dinosaurs and birds.

FAST FACTS

The wing feathers of many bird-like dinosaurs seem to have been black — this pigment is known to make feathers stronger. The fossil feathers of *Caihong*, found in northern China in 2014, also contain evidence that they were iridescent, like the dark feathers of starlings.

Black feathers are stronger than pale ones, so they may have been adapted for flight.

Microscopic analysis shows that the head and neck glowed with iridescent colour.

Living animals have colours that help them survive. The same would have applied to dinosaurs, and many smaller ones were probably camouflaged to help them hide from enemies. The hair-like feathers of the small hunter *Sinosauropteryx* contain traces of colour cells that seem to show counter-shading – the pale belly and dark back that disguise the shapes of living animals such as deer. But feathers can be much brighter colours than this, and it is possible that some small feathered hunters looked more like vividly coloured birds.

Microscopic clues indicate that *Sinosauropteryx* had a dark orange-brown back.

The tail seems to have been striped, like the tail of a raccoon.

The underside was much paler in colour.

SINOSAUROPTERYX LIVED 125 MYA IN THE FORESTS OF CHINA, WHERE IT PREYED ON SMALL ANIMALS.

THIS SMALL HUNTER WAS THE FIRST NON-FLYING DINOSAUR TO BE FOUND WITH FOSSIL EVIDENCE OF SIMPLE FEATHERS.

WHAT COLOUR
WERE DINOSAURS?

Most of our knowledge of extinct dinosaurs is based on their fossilized bones, which cannot preserve any evidence of colour. So, knowing that dinosaurs were reptiles, scientists assumed they would have looked like modern reptiles such as lizards. But we now know that many dinosaurs had feathers, which can be much more colourful. What's more, some fossilized feathers and skin contain microscopic structures that may indicate what colour they were when the animals were alive.

Some dinosaurs could have been as colourful as a modern parrot.

COLOUR CLUES

Some fossil feathers preserve the remains of microscopic structures that give the feathers their colour. The shapes of these melanosomes may indicate what colour they produced — provided they were not altered by the fossilization process.

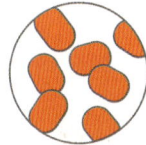

Rust

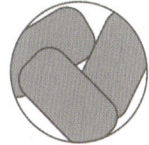

Grey

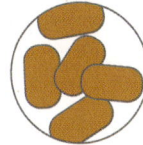

Brown

Black

Iridescent

FOSSILS OF THE BIRD-LIKE *ANCHIORNIS* SHOW THAT IT HAD RED, GREY, BLACK, AND WHITE FEATHERS.

EVIDENCE OF COLOUR HAS ALSO BEEN FOUND IN THE SKIN AND SCALES OF *PSITTACOSAURUS*.

FAST FACTS

In 2020, a tiny skull was discovered in a lump of amber 99 million years old. Called *Oculudentavis*, it was thought to be the smallest-ever dinosaur. But when scientists took another look, they realized the skull belonged to a lizard.

Found in the 1850s, the chicken-sized skeleton of a young *Compsognathus* was the first evidence that not all dinosaurs were lumbering giants. Even full-grown adult *Compsognathus* were no bigger than turkeys.

The bee hummingbird is the **smallest** known dinosaur.

Like other birds, a pigeon is a dinosaur adapted for flight.

WHAT'S THE
SMALLEST DINOSAUR?

We usually think of dinosaurs as colossal animals that shook the ground with every footstep. But many of the extinct dinosaurs that ran around the feet of these giants were no bigger than crows or pigeons. And since we now know that crows, pigeons, and all other birds are in fact living dinosaurs, some of the smallest dinosaurs that ever lived are flying around our heads right now. They include sparrows, colourful songbirds, and tiny iridescent hummingbirds.

TINY BIRDS NOT MUCH BIGGER THAN THE BEE HUMMINGBIRD WERE IN FLIGHT 113 MYA.

THE **BODY OF A BEE HUMMINGBIRD** IS NO BIGGER THAN THAT OF A QUEEN BUMBLEBEE.

FRAGILE BONES

Most fossil dinosaur bones are those of big animals. This is because they were more likely to survive than the bones of small dinosaurs. In fact, dinosaurs even smaller than *Anchiornis* were probably very common, like flocks of birds today, but their remains were destroyed by decay or other animals long before they could be fossilized. Only a few fossil sites around the world preserve the delicate remains of very small dinosaurs.

Fossil skeleton of *Anchiornis*

The bee hummingbird flaps its wings 80 times a second.

The wings of *Anchiornis* were not strong enough for flight, but it might have been able to glide.

At just 6 cm (2.4 in) long, and weighing only 2 g (0.07 oz), the bee hummingbird of Cuba is probably the smallest bird that ever lived. This makes it the smallest dinosaur, unless scientists find an extinct one that was even smaller. One of the smallest extinct dinosaurs found so far is *Anchiornis*, a pigeon-sized feathered hunter that lived in China 160 MYA. Although it looked very like a bird, it probably could not fly.

THE NAME *ANCHIORNIS* MEANS "NEAR BIRD", REFERRING TO THE FACT THAT IT WAS COVERED IN FEATHERS.

250

ANCHIORNIS PROBABLY WEIGHED UP TO 250 G (8.8 OZ) – THE WEIGHT OF A HAMSTER.

The curved frill accounted for one-third of its length.

The two large holes may have helped keep the skull lightweight.

These horns jutted out from the skull.

Short nose horn

Torosaurus used its parrot-like beak to rip away tough vegetation.

Torosaurus **had the largest** skull of any known land animal.

1891

TOROSAURUS **FOSSILS** WERE FIRST DISCOVERED IN 1891 IN WESTERN USA.

CERATOPSIANS SURVIVED TO THE VERY END OF THE MESOZOIC ERA.

WHICH DINOSAUR HAD THE
LARGEST SKULL?

Ceratopsians were a group of plant-eating dinosaurs known for their formidable horned heads. They included the elephant-sized *Triceratops*, named for the three long horns on its gigantic skull. But the skull of *Torosaurus* was even bigger, with an extra-long bony frill at the back. Some scientists have suggested that they were the same animal, with *Triceratops* turning into *Torosaurus* as it got older. But others think they were separate species that happened to live at the same time and place.

Torosaurus **could grow** to 9 m (30 ft) long, and weighed about 6 tonnes (7 tons). It was a slow mover and would have been tempting prey for big predators like the fearsome *Tyrannosaurus*, which lived at the same time. *Torosaurus* had a massive shield-like skull, which at almost 3 m (10 ft) was about the same height as a basketball hoop. The extended frill in the top may have been used to attract a mate, while the two long, sharp horns above its eyes would have helped to fend off predators.

FRILLED DEFENCE

Some animals alive today use frills as a form of defence. When threatened, the frilled lizard from Australia and New Guinea stands on its hind legs, unfurls a colourful flap of skin around its neck, and opens its mouth wide. The neck frill makes it look much larger than it is, scaring predators away.

The lizard hisses as it opens its brightly coloured mouth.

A CAST OF *TOROSAURUS* AT THE DENVER MUSEUM OF NATURE AND SCIENCE, USA, IS NICKNAMED **TINY**.

THE ANIMAL WITH THE **LARGEST SKULL** TODAY IS THE SPERM WHALE.

The **horns** were about 1.2 m (4 ft) in length – about the same as the average 12-year-old.

FRILLED GIANT

Torosaurus was a huge, spectacular animal. Its elaborate skull was almost certainly partly for defence against the tyrannosaurs that lived alongside it, but it may also have been partly for show. If brightly coloured, the frill would have looked dramatic, and may have been used like the antlers of modern deer to impress rivals and attract breeding partners. The animals with the biggest, most colourful frills would have had more breeding success than their rivals, and therefore more young.

DID DINOSAURS
LIVE IN BURROWS?

Many modern animals rest or breed underground in burrows. They include mammals, reptiles, and even some birds. But the plant-eating *Oryctodromeus* is the only extinct dinosaur known to have lived like this. In 2007, the fossilized remains of three of these animals were discovered inside a burrow that they almost certainly dug themselves. Other dinosaurs probably did the same, but so far we have no proof.

BURROWING BIRDS

The burrow made by *Oryctodromeus* was similar to those made by some modern birds, which — like all birds — are living relatives of dinosaurs. Some modern birds nest in burrows to keep their eggs and young safe from predators. But a burrow also provides shelter from extreme weather, especially in hot climates where it retains moisture and keeps the temperature constant.

Atlantic puffins are ocean birds that return to land to breed. Some take over the clifftop burrows of rabbits. Others use their beaks and sharp claws to dig their own, lining the nest chamber with grass and feathers. The result is very similar to the burrow made by *Oryctodromeus*.

Atlantic puffin

The American burrowing owl lives in dry regions with few trees, so it nests and shelters in a burrow. It usually adopts one dug by some other animal, but may dig its own. If an enemy tries to get into its burrow, the owl scares it away by imitating the warning rattle and hiss of a venomous rattlesnake.

Burrowing owl

When it was time to leave its parents, a young *Oryctodromeus* would dig its own burrow or moved into an empty one.

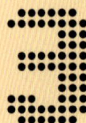

THE FOSSILS OF THREE *ORYCTODROMEUS* IN THEIR BURROW WERE FOUND IN MONTANA, USA, IN 2007.

THE *ORYCTODROMEUS* FAMILY PROBABLY DROWNED WHEN THEIR BURROW WAS FLOODED DURING A STORM.

The young lived with the adults until they were able to fend for themselves.

The burrow containing the fossilized bones of *Oryctodromeus* was about the same width as the adult animal, showing that it had made the burrow itself. Two juveniles were found in the burrow alongside the adult, and it is likely that they hatched from eggs laid in an underground nursery chamber.

Hidden in the burrow, the eggs would have been safe from bigger dinosaurs that might steal and eat them.

When it was ready to hatch, the baby dinosaur used the tip of its beak to break the eggshell.

ORYCTODROMEUS RAN ON ITS TWO BACK LEGS, ENABLING ITS HANDS TO BE ADAPTED FOR **EFFICIENT DIGGING**.

DIGGING A **BURROW** MIGHT HAVE HELPED THIS DINOSAUR LIVE IN A HOT, NORMALLY DRY CLIMATE.

Dinosaur data

EARTH CLOCK

It can be hard to imagine just how long ago dinosaurs lived. Take a look at Earth's history compressed into **24 hours.** Each second represents **5,000 years.**

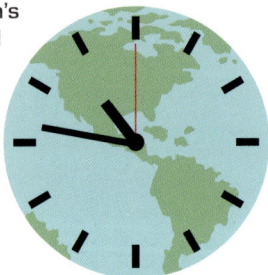

00:00
At midnight, Earth forms from a swirling mass of dust and gases.

04:26
Life originates on Earth with simple lifeforms on the seafloor.

21:08
An explosion of new animals takes place in the seas.

21:30
Plants appear on land. These were, at first, simple moss-like organisms.

22:47
Dinosaurs evolve on land and dominate life.

Six seconds to midnight
Our species, *Homo sapiens*, appears in Africa.

STRANGE BUT TRUE

▲ *Pegomastax*
No bigger than a house cat, this plant-eating dinosaur had a parrot-like beak, huge canine teeth, and porcupine-like quills. It lived during the Jurassic Period in southern Africa.

▶ *Yi qi*
Yi qi looked more like a bat than a dinosaur. With its wings outstretched, *Yi qi* may have glided from tree to tree like a modern-day flying squirrel. As well as sharp toe claws, it had claws at the end of its wings.

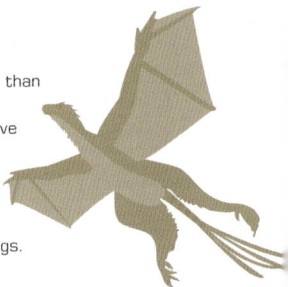

▶ *Linhenykus*
This peculiar creature is the only known one-fingered dinosaur. The size of a small dog, it may have used its clawed finger for raiding ant and termite nests during the Late Cretaceous period.

ALTHOUGH THERE ARE THREE MAIN GROUPS OF DINOSAUR, HUNDREDS OF SPECIES EXISTED WITHIN EACH GROUP.

THEROPODS EVOLVED IN THE TRIASSIC. THEY WERE SMALL AND AGILE HUNTERS.

DINOSAUR DIETS

▲ Carnivores
Meat-eating dinosaurs preyed on any animal, including other dinosaurs. They came in all sizes — from the cat-sized *Microraptor* to the bus-sized *Gigantosaurus*.

▲ Herbivores
These dinosaurs munched on leaves, grasses, and seeds. Unlike carnivores who usually had one large meal a day, herbivores ate all day long.

▲ Omnivores
There were a few dinosaurs that ate both plants and meat. They are known as omnivores. They ate anything, including insects, plants, and even other dinosaurs.

ON THE MOVE

Just like modern-day birds and some mammals, some plant-eating dinosaurs embarked on long journeys when food became scarce.

Camarasaurus travelled up to 300 km (190 miles) in Late Jurassic North America in search of food and water, and then back again when the season changed.

During the Late Cretaceous, *Pachyrhinosaurus* migrated 3,500 km (2,200 miles) north from Alberta, Canada, to the Arctic to feed on new sources of food. They migrated south again when the Arctic winter set in.

DINOSAUR DEFENCES

From butting heads to clubbed tails and claws, dinosaurs developed novel ways to protect themselves in the **Mesozoic Era.**

▶ Huge head
Pachycephalosaurus's skull was **20 times thicker** than any other dinosaur. The super strong skull may have been used to **head-butt** anyone who tried to attack it.

▶ Club tail
Euoplocephalus's tail had a huge club at the end of it. The club was made out of **chunks of bone** fused together and would have been powerful enough to **break bone.**

▶ Camouflage
A dinosaur from China called *Psittacosaurus* had **light skin on its belly and darker skin on its back**, helping it to blend in with its forest habitat and making it harder for predators to detect.

CAMARASAURUS IS THE MOST COMMONLY FOUND DINOSAUR FROM THE LATE JURASSIC IN NORTH AMERICA.

1.8

SATURNALIA, AN ANCESTOR OF SAUROPODS, WAS ONLY ABOUT 1.8 M (6 FT) LONG.

Dinosaur biology

The fossilized remains of extinct dinosaurs are mostly bones and teeth, but they can tell us a lot about how the bodies of these astonishing animals worked, what they ate, and how they lived and died.

The gigantic, massively strong teeth and jaws of *Tyrannosaurus* made it the most powerful land predator of all time. Only the fastest-running or most heavily armoured prey could hope to survive if it launched an attack on them.

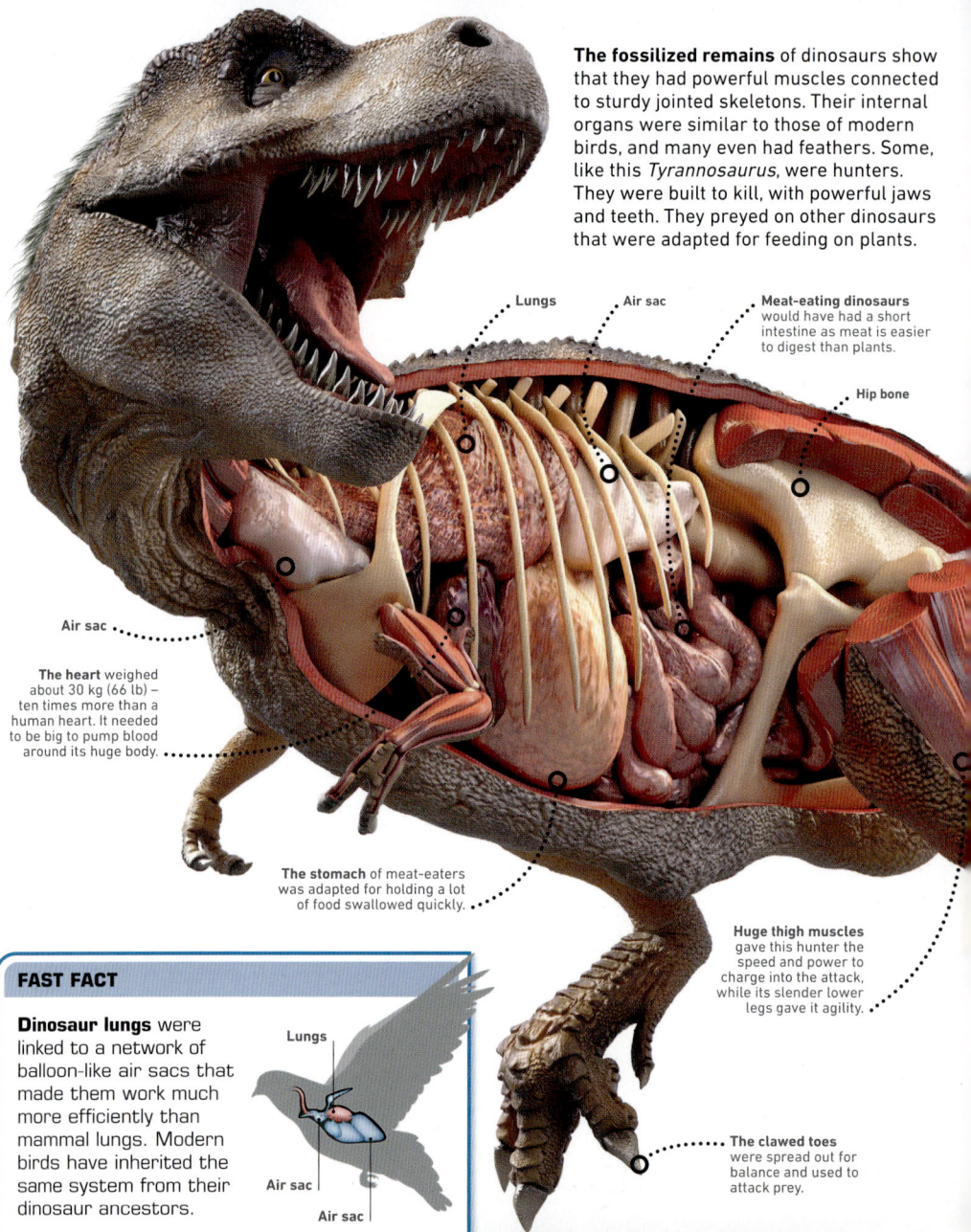

The fossilized remains of dinosaurs show that they had powerful muscles connected to sturdy jointed skeletons. Their internal organs were similar to those of modern birds, and many even had feathers. Some, like this *Tyrannosaurus*, were hunters. They were built to kill, with powerful jaws and teeth. They preyed on other dinosaurs that were adapted for feeding on plants.

Lungs

Air sac

Meat-eating dinosaurs would have had a short intestine as meat is easier to digest than plants.

Hip bone

Air sac

The heart weighed about 30 kg (66 lb) – ten times more than a human heart. It needed to be big to pump blood around its huge body.

The stomach of meat-eaters was adapted for holding a lot of food swallowed quickly.

Huge thigh muscles gave this hunter the speed and power to charge into the attack, while its slender lower legs gave it agility.

The clawed toes were spread out for balance and used to attack prey.

FAST FACT

Dinosaur lungs were linked to a network of balloon-like air sacs that made them work much more efficiently than mammal lungs. Modern birds have inherited the same system from their dinosaur ancestors.

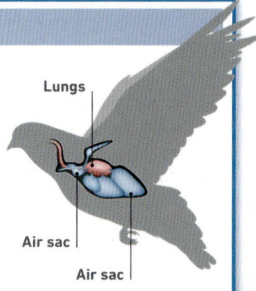

Lungs

Air sac

Air sac

DINOSAURS WERE REPTILES, LIKE LIZARDS, BUT WITH MANY OF THE FEATURES OF BIRDS.

THE BONES, MUSCLES, AND INTERNAL ORGANS OF DINOSAURS WERE JUST AS EFFICIENT AS THOSE OF MODERN ANIMALS.

INSIDE A PLANT-EATER

Many dinosaurs ate plants such as ferns and the tough leaves of conifer trees. These foods take much longer to digest than meat, so the plant-eaters needed much bigger digestive systems than meat-eaters. Some — the biggest — supported the extra weight on four stout limbs. Others, like this *Iguanodon*, had strong forelimbs that they could use for support when they needed to.

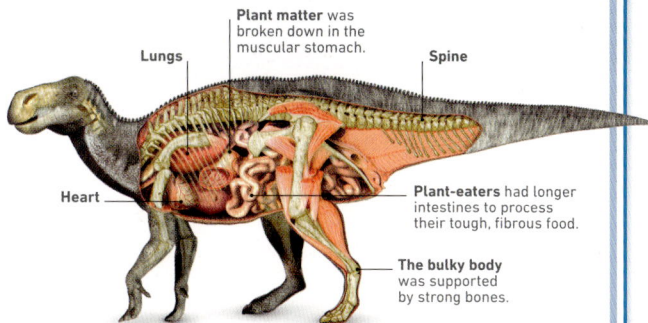

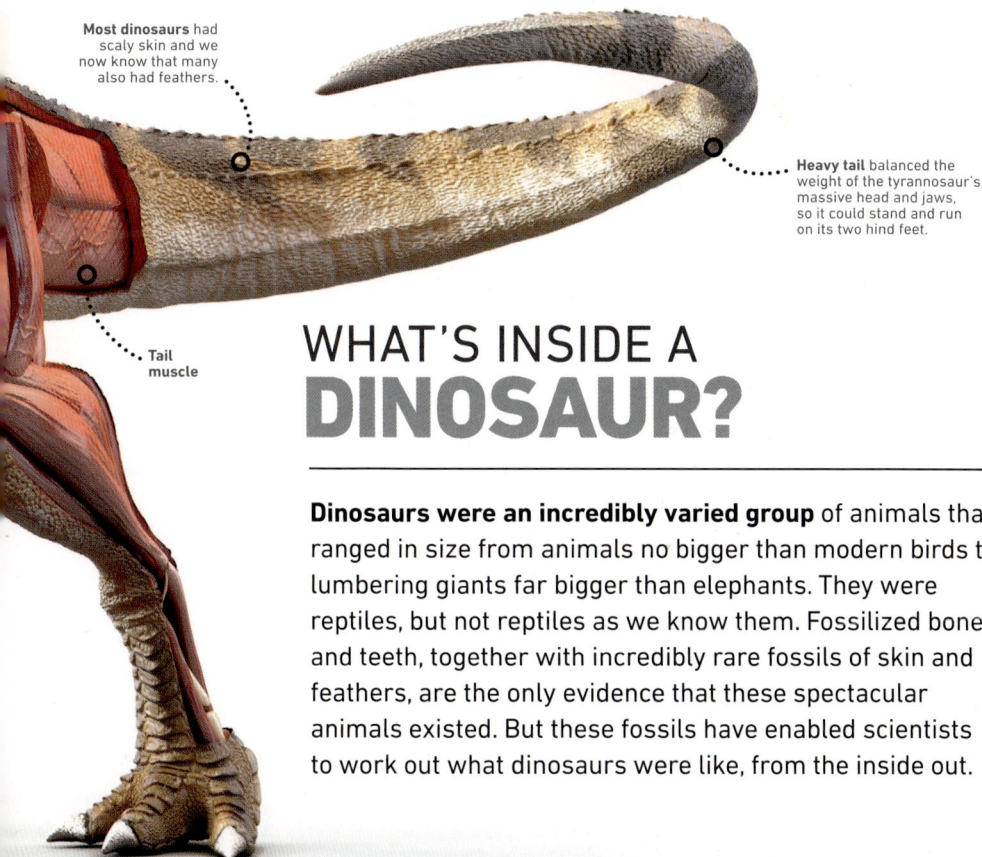

Plant matter was broken down in the muscular stomach.

Lungs

Spine

Heart

Plant-eaters had longer intestines to process their tough, fibrous food.

The bulky body was supported by strong bones.

Most dinosaurs had scaly skin and we now know that many also had feathers.

Heavy tail balanced the weight of the tyrannosaur's massive head and jaws, so it could stand and run on its two hind feet.

Tail muscle

WHAT'S INSIDE A
DINOSAUR?

Dinosaurs were an incredibly varied group of animals that ranged in size from animals no bigger than modern birds to lumbering giants far bigger than elephants. They were reptiles, but not reptiles as we know them. Fossilized bones and teeth, together with incredibly rare fossils of skin and feathers, are the only evidence that these spectacular animals existed. But these fossils have enabled scientists to work out what dinosaurs were like, from the inside out.

THE **VISION** OF HUNTERS LIKE TYRANNOSAURS MAY HAVE BEEN AS ACUTE AS AN EAGLE'S.

FEATHERS EVOLVED TO KEEP DINOSAURS WARM. MILLIONS OF YEARS LATER, BIRDS ADAPTED THEM FOR FLIGHT.

Weighing up to **70 tonnes** (77 tons), *Patagotitan* is one of the largest species of titanosaur discovered so far. It used its incredibly long neck to reach the tops of trees to continually feed on leaves. In a single day, this heavyweight dinosaur consumed at least 250 kg (550 lb) of plant material.

Patagotitan ate a **skip full of plants** every day to get enough nutrients.

Like scissors, the small teeth nipped the leaves from trees so that the food could be gulped down.

HOW MUCH COULD
PATAGOTITAN EAT?

This colossal creature belonged to a group of giant plant-eating dinosaurs called titanosaurs, meaning "titanic lizards". *Patagotitan* was the same length as three double-decker buses and weighed as much as 15 African elephants. It roamed the arid plains of modern-day Argentina during the Late Cretaceous period in search of plants to fuel its immense body.

THE **STOMACH** OF *PATAGOTITAN* WEIGHED AS MUCH AS A HIPPOPOTAMUS.

50 *PATAGOTITAN'S* **INTESTINE** MAY HAVE BEEN AS LONG AS 50 M (164 FT).

FAST FACTS

In 2008, while looking for his lost sheep, a farmer in Patagonia in southern Argentina saw a huge object sticking out from the ground. It turned out to be a 2.4 m (8 ft) long *Patagotitan* thigh bone.

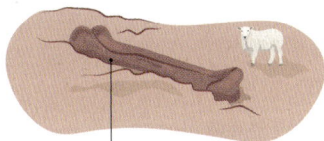

Over millions of years, the wind and rain had worn away the surrounding rock.

Food stayed in a titanosaur's stomach for about 11 days to extract as many nutrients as possible. The bacteria in the gut helped it digest the tough food.

THIS DINOSAUR BROWSED ON THE LEAVES OF THE MONKEY PUZZLE TREE, *ARAUCARIA*. IT STILL GROWS IN PATAGONIA TODAY.

PATAGOTITAN WINS THE TITLE FOR THE **BIGGEST POO** – EACH POO WAS AS HEAVY AS A DACHSHUND DOG.

HOW MUCH BLOOD COULD A
SAUROPOD'S HEART PUMP?

The heart is a machine like no other, whether it is powering the tiny insect-eating dinosaur *Anchiornis* or gigantic sauropods like *Argentinosaurus*. But the bigger the dinosaur, the bigger this powerful organ needed to be. A fossilized sauropod heart has never been discovered so scientists have to look at living animals to find out how it may have worked.

POWERFUL PUMP

Both crocodiles and birds, which are relatives of dinosaurs, have four-chambered hearts, so it is likely that sauropods did too, and they would have worked in a similar way — the left and right sides beat together to push the blood around the body and then back to the lungs again to pick up oxygen.

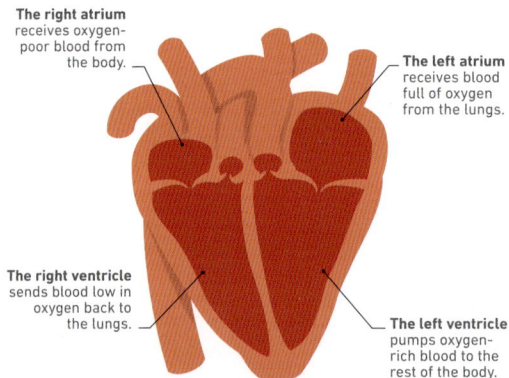

The right atrium receives oxygen-poor blood from the body.

The left atrium receives blood full of oxygen from the lungs.

The right ventricle sends blood low in oxygen back to the lungs.

The left ventricle pumps oxygen-rich blood to the rest of the body.

AT 230 KG (500 LB), A SAUROPOD'S HEART WEIGHED AS MUCH AS A MALE GRIZZLY BEAR.

A SAUROPOD'S BLOOD VESSELS MAY HAVE BEEN BIG ENOUGH FOR A SMALL CHILD TO CRAWL THROUGH.

The biggest **sauropod heart** pumped about 90 litres (160 pints) of blood per heartbeat.

FAST FACTS

Octopuses and squid have three hearts. The main heart pumps blood around the body; the other two pump blood to the gills. They also have blue blood.

Some skinks on the island of Papua New Guinea have green blood. This makes their heart green as well as their muscles, bones, and tongue.

Giraffes have strong heart muscles in their left ventricle, which is used to force blood up their neck and back into their brain when they lift their head, stopping any dizziness.

Scientists have estimated that *Patagotitan* would have pumped blood every five seconds – that's 12 beats per minute. Its heart would have been colossal because it needed to be powerful enough to pump blood around its massive body.

THE HEART OF A **BLUE WHALE** WEIGHS ABOUT 200 KG (440 LB) – THE LARGEST OF ANY LIVING ANIMAL.

THE SMALLEST LIVING DINOSAUR IS THE **BEE HUMMINGBIRD**. ITS TINY HEART BEATS 1,260 TIMES A MINUTE.

WHAT WAS THE
FASTEST DINOSAUR?

Known as "ostrich dinosaurs", ornithomimids were feathered theropods with toothless beaks. They first appeared during the Early Cretaceous in what is now North America and Asia. They were much larger than the modern-day ostrich and could easily outrun other dinosaurs. By contrast, heavily armoured dinosaurs like *Stegosaurus* plodded along at a jogging speed of a human.

Many two-legged hunters such as *Tyrannosaurus* would have been quick movers, and despite its huge size, scientists estimate that *Tyrannosaurus* would have been able to reach speeds of 20 kph (12 mph).

The fastest runners in the world can sprint at speeds of up to 44 kph (27 mph).

Built like a tank and armed with a spiked tail, *Stegosaurus* didn't need to rely on speed to escape from predators – it probably couldn't move faster than 11 kph (7 mph).

Ornithomimus was the **fastest** of any dinosaur and could outrun a racehorse.

Velociraptor, meaning "swift thief", was light and agile, and could easily catch most prey, running in short bursts of 40 kph (25 mph).

ORNITHOMIMUS COULD RUN THE LENGTH OF A FOOTBALL PITCH IN JUST OVER 5 SECONDS.

THE FASTEST LAND ANIMAL TODAY IS THE CHEETAH, SPRINTING AT SPEEDS OF ALMOST 112 KPH (70 MPH).

FAST FACTS

Gallimimus was the largest and heaviest of the ornithomimids — at 440 kg (970 lb), it weighed as much as a grand piano.

The long tail may have helped the dinosaur to balance its weight while running at high speed.

The fastest bird on Earth today is the ostrich. Reaching speeds of up to 70 kph (43 mph), it relies on its sprinting skills to escape from predators or, if cornered, it lashes out with its powerful legs.

A single ostrich kick is powerful enough to kill a predator.

With a lightweight body, long hind limbs, and powerful leg muscles, ornithomimids were built for speed. The fastest was *Ornithomimus* – at about 3.5 m (12 ft) long, it was also one of the smallest of the ostrich dinosaurs. These feathered dinosaurs used their toes to dig into the ground while running – like spikes on running shoes. They needed all the help they could get to outrun their main predator – the tyrannosaurs.

Scientists estimate that *Ornithomimus* reached a top speed of 80 kph (50 mph).

The long legs were slim, similar to the legs of all fast-running animals today.

WHICH DINOSAUR HAD THE
LONGEST TAIL?

Diplodocus **was a sauropod** and one of the largest animals to have ever lived. It had a whip-like tail, which it may have used for balance. But as this colossal plant-eater could not have moved very fast, plodding along at a top speed of only 15 kph (9 mph), it may also have used its long tail to defend itself, lashing out at any creature that dared to come near. At about 14 m (46 ft) in length – the size of a small jet plane – it had the longest tail of any known land animal.

Diplodocus **had the longest tail of any animal on Earth.**

Diplodocus may have held its tail above the ground as a counterbalance to its long neck.

33 *DIPLODOCUS* WAS ABOUT 33 M (108 FT) LONG – MOST OF THIS LENGTH WAS MADE UP BY ITS NECK AND TAIL.

>> *DIPLODOCUS* MEANS "DOUBLE BEAM" IN GREEK, REFERRING TO THE CHEVRON-SHAPED BONES UNDER ITS TAIL.

FAST FACTS

In 2016, palaeontologists found evidence of a feathered dinosaur tail preserved in a 99-million-year-old lump of amber. The tail belonged to a coelurosaur, a meat-eating dinosaur that was the size of a sparrow.

The tail feathers were brown.

This Late Cretaceous plant-eating dinosaur, called *Stegouros*, had a formidable weapon — a short but bladed tail that looked like an Aztec war club. It also had fewer tail bones than other armoured dinosaurs.

The tail was lined with flat, bony plates used for slashing enemies.

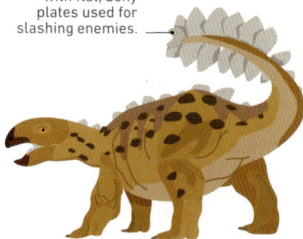

Shunosaurus, a slow-moving sauropod from Jurassic China, had an effective weapon against predators — a bony clubbed tail with small spikes jutting out.

The tail spikes were made of osteoderms — bones that were embedded in the skin.

Fossil evidence suggests that *Diplodocus* had a row of thin, bony spines along its neck, back, and tail.

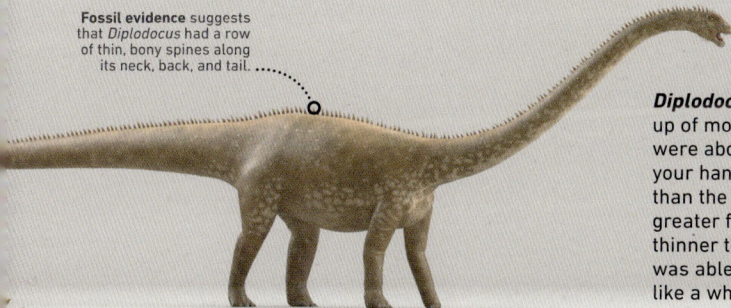

Diplodocus's colossal tail was made up of more than 80 bones — some were about the size of the palm of your hand. These bones were shorter than the neck bones, allowing for greater flexibility. With a tail that was thinner towards the tip, a *Diplodocus* was able to wield the end of its tail like a whip, producing a deafening crack that broke the sound barrier.

THE TIP OF ITS TAIL MAY HAVE MOVED AT 1,200 KPH (745 MPH) — **FASTER** THAN AN AEROPLANE.

AT 2.4 M (8 FT) IN LENGTH, THE **GIRAFFE** HAS THE LONGEST TAIL OF ANY LIVING ANIMAL.

Diplodocus had **356 bones** – an adult human skeleton consists of 206 bones.

DIPPY

This 26-m (85-ft) long skeleton of *Diplodocus* has been on display at the Natural History Museum in London for more than 100 years, making it one of the world's best-known dinosaurs. Named Dippy, the skeleton is made up of casts of the original dinosaur bones discovered in Wyoming, USA, in 1898. Originally the long tail was reconstructed trailing on the ground, but we now think *Diplodocus* would have carried it much higher to balance its long neck.

Tyrannosaurus had the most **powerful bite** of any land animal.

Tyrannosaurus was about 13 m (43 ft) long.

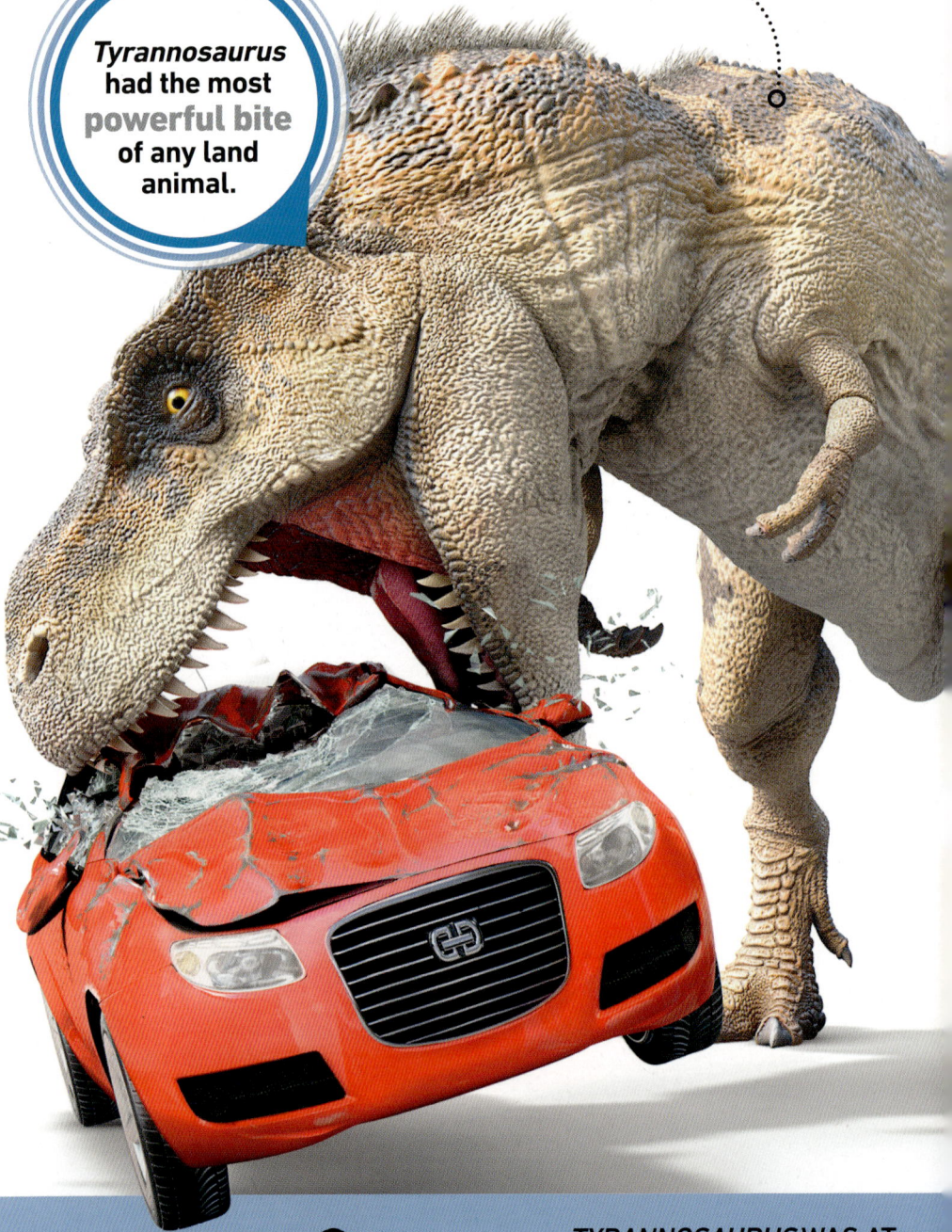

TYRANNOSAURUS WAS AT THE **TOP OF THE FOOD CHAIN** – IT DIDN'T NEED TO FEAR ANY ANIMAL APART FROM ANOTHER *TYRANNOSAURUS.*

WHICH DINOSAUR HAD THE
MOST POWERFUL BITE?

Tyrannosaurus **was one of the deadliest** land predators that has ever existed. It roamed the forests and open land of North America towards the very end of the Mesozoic Era, on the prowl for its next victim. Armed with a lethal weapon – colossal jaws that were equipped with huge teeth – this terrifying hunter could cripple almost any prey that crossed its path.

The muscular tail helped to counterbalance its heavy head.

FORMIDABLE JAWS

Massive muscles moved the powerful jaws and gave *Tyrannosaurus* its deadly bite. Chomping through flesh, muscle, and bone, *Tyrannosaurus* ripped off chunks of meat and swallowed them whole.

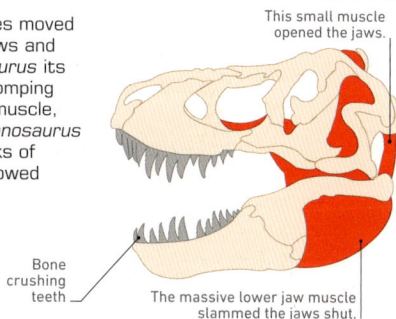

This small muscle opened the jaws.

Bone crushing teeth

The massive lower jaw muscle slammed the jaws shut.

Although some carnivorous dinosaurs were about the same size as *Tyrannosaurus*, none of them had a more lethal bite than this dinosaur. As well as being equipped with immensely powerful jaw muscles, it also had incredibly strong neck muscles that made for a bone-shattering bite – one that would have been powerful enough to crush a small car.

FAST FACTS

By studying the jawbones and muscles of animals, scientists can work out the bite force of animals. Today, the great white shark is estimated to have a bite force of 18,000 newtons (N) — possibly the strongest in the living animal kingdom. But the bite force of *Tyrannosaurus* may have between 35,000 and 60,000 newtons — more than double the strength of the great white.

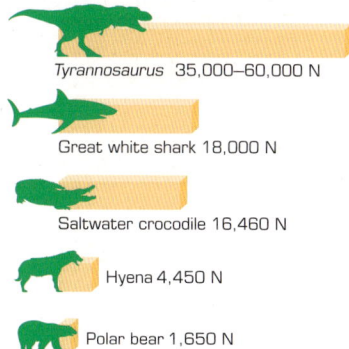

Tyrannosaurus   35,000–60,000 N

Great white shark 18,000 N

Saltwater crocodile 16,460 N

Hyena 4,450 N

Polar bear 1,650 N

SOME TYRANNOSAURS WERE INFECTED BY TINY PARASITES THAT ATE AWAY THE SOFT TISSUES OF THE THROAT AND JAWS.

RELATIVE TO ITS BODY SIZE, THE TINY GALÁPAGOS GROUND FINCH HAS A BITE FORCE 320 TIMES GREATER THAN *TYRANNOSAURUS*.

WHICH DINOSAUR HAD THE
LONGEST TEETH?

Dinosaur teeth come in all shapes and sizes. By studying the teeth of a dinosaur, it is possible to work out what and how it would have eaten. For example, those dinosaurs with sharp, curved, and serrated teeth are typical of meat-eating dinosaurs. Of all the dinosaur teeth that are known, *Tyrannosaurus* takes the title for the longest. Its jaws were full of banana-sized teeth that were capable of crunching bone.

FAST FACTS

While carnivores had sharp blade-like teeth for tearing meat, herbivores had flat teeth for grinding tough plants. Others, including *Deinocheirus* were toothless, relying on their beaks for snipping plants.

Toothless beak

Deinocheirus

Like meat-eating dinosaurs, living crocodiles replace their old teeth when they wear out. Crocodiles can get through at least 3,000 teeth during their lifetime.

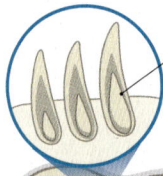

A crocodile's new tooth grows inside the old, hollow tooth.

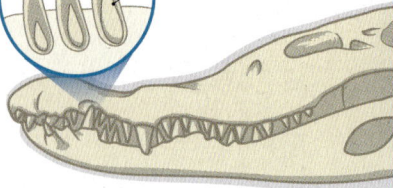

Tyrannosaurus **had the longest teeth of any dinosaur.**

AS WELL AS THE LONGEST, *T. REX* HAD SOME OF THE STRONGEST TEETH OF ANY MEAT-EATING DINOSAUR.

EVIDENCE OF *T. REX* MUNCHING BONE COMES FROM FRAGMENTS FOUND IN FOSSILIZED *T. REX* POO (COPROLITES).

Tyrannosaurus's powerful jaws were lined with huge teeth of different sizes. The longest of these were 20 cm (8 in). They were sharp and saw-edged, enabling *Tyrannosaurus* to slice through tough skin and muscle. But they were also deep-rooted, making them strong enough to bite through bone without snapping off.

DEADLY CLASHES

Tyrannosaurus's specialized teeth enabled it to attack any prey, including the largest of the horned dinosaurs, *Triceratops*. Palaeontologists have found a number of fossilized bones belonging to *Triceratops* that have bite marks matching the teeth of a *Tyrannosaurus*. Bite marks have also been found on neck frills, suggesting that *Tyrannosaurus* may have tried to get at a *Triceratops's* meaty neck muscles.

Triceratops and Tyrannosaurus

NOT ALL **ATTACKS** WERE DEADLY. FOSSILS OF SEVERAL PLANT-EATING DINOSAURS SHOW HEALED *T. REX* BITE MARKS.

T. REX'S **TOOTH-STUDDED JAW** WAS ABOUT 120 CM (4 FT) LONG.

WHICH DINOSAUR HAD THE
MOST TEETH?

The number of teeth in a dinosaur's jaws varied from species to species. Those dinosaurs with the most efficient teeth were the so-called "duckbilled" dinosaurs, the hadrosaurs like *Edmontosaurus*, which had beaks that resembled those of a duck. The hadrosaurs were a very successful group of plant-eating dinosaurs that lived during the Cretaceous Period. They had teeth that were far more efficient and complex than modern grazers.

FAST FACTS

Sharks have multiple rows of teeth in their jaws. These teeth are continually replaced. Some sharks go through as many as 30,000 teeth in a lifetime.

The whale shark has 300 rows of tiny teeth, which are no bigger than the size of a match head. It also has teeth-like structures on its body. These help it to glide through water.

On land, the giant armadillo has the highest number of teeth for a mammal — up to 100.

A **hadrosaur** had 30 times as many teeth as a human.

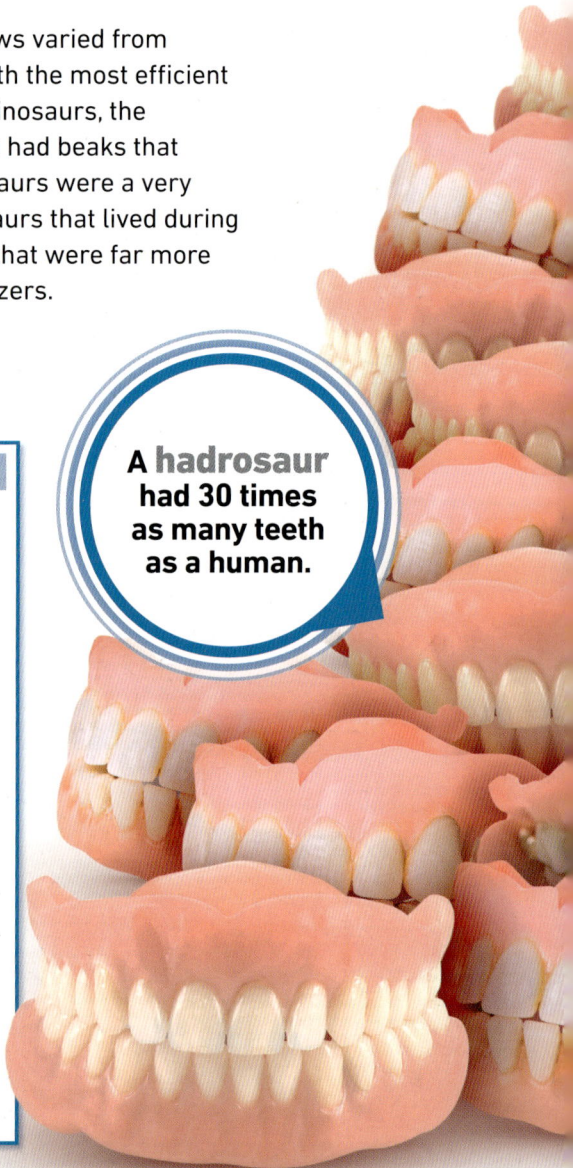

MOST PLANT-EATERS HAD SIMPLE **LEAF-SHAPED TEETH** WITH SERRATED EDGES.

AN ANCIENT FISH CALLED *HELICOPRION* HAD A SPIRAL CLUSTER OF TEETH IN ITS JAWS, CALLED A TOOTH WHORL.

Adult humans have 32 teeth but hadrosaurs had as many as 1,000 tiny teeth in their jaws – that's more than 30 times as many teeth as a human. Hadrosaurs had the most complex teeth of any dinosaur, being made of six distinct types of tissue – modern grazers like horses and cows only have four types.

GRINDERS

Hadrosaur teeth were contained inside a "dental battery", where rows of hundreds of teeth were stacked on top of each other. As the teeth wore down, they were replaced throughout the animal's lifetime. These tooth batteries were angled in such a way that allowed the dinosaurs to grind tough vegetation into an easily digestible pulp.

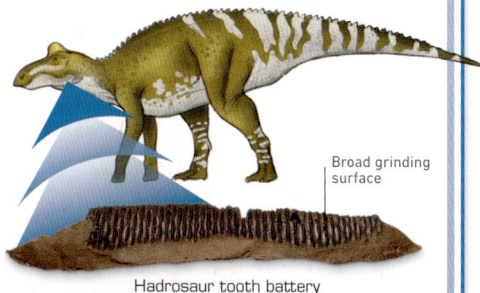

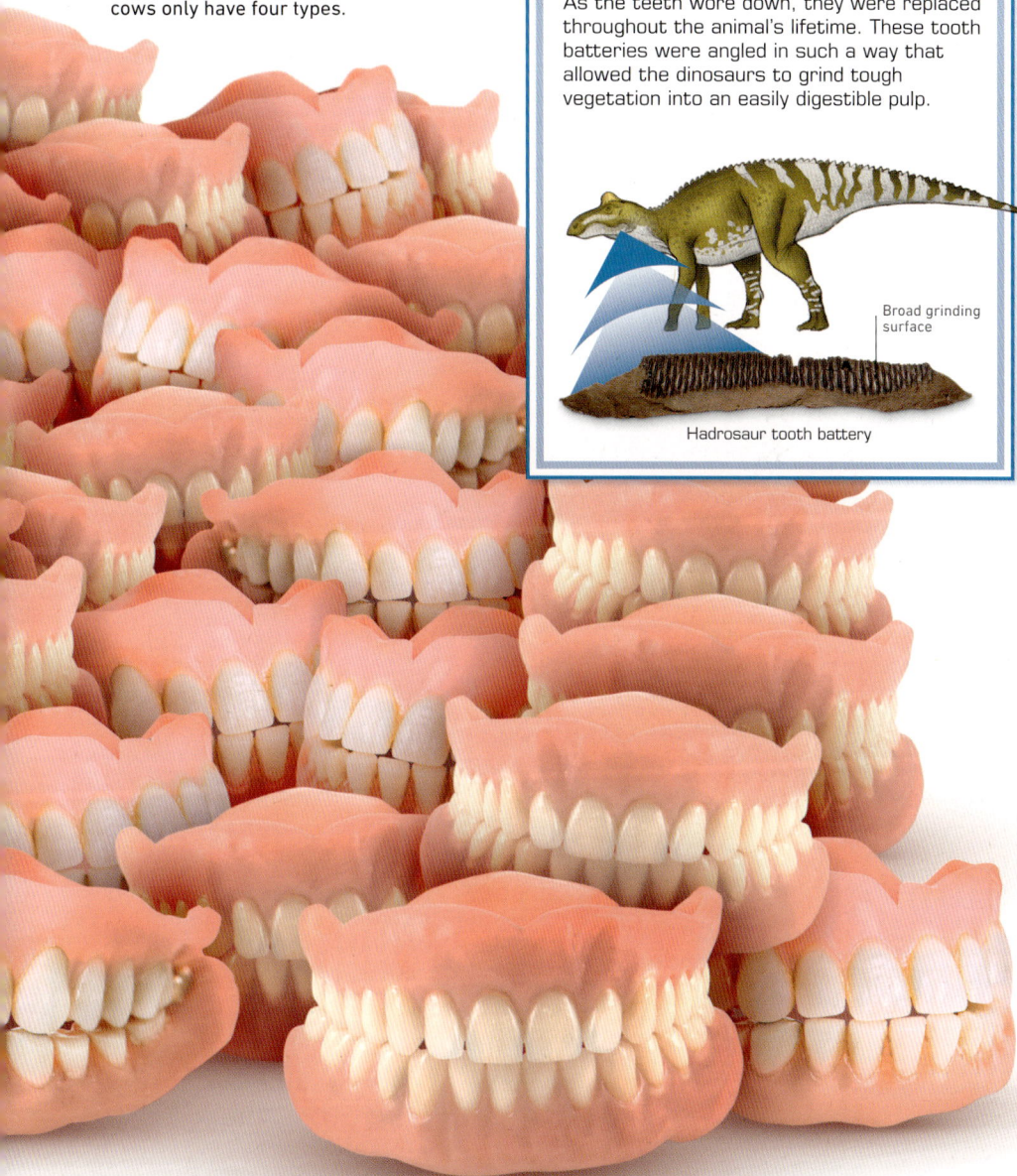

Broad grinding surface

Hadrosaur tooth battery

THE MALE, PIG-LIKE BABIRUSA HAS CANINES THAT CURVE UP AND BACKWARDS, WHICH MAY PIERCE ITS FACE.

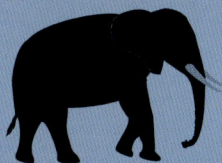

THE GIANT TUSKS OF ELEPHANTS ARE ACTUALLY EXTRA-LONG INCISOR TEETH.

Therizinosaurus had the longest claws of any animal.

Each bony claw would have been covered with a horn-like keratin sheath, making it even longer.

Fingers

Giraffe-sized *Therizinosaurus* had the longest claws of any known animal – extinct or living. The longest claw was about 50 cm (20 in), longer than a house cat. As well as using them for gathering plants, the massive claws may have been used to defend itself – *Therizinosaurus* had short legs and probably could not outrun predators.

WHEN *THERIZINOSAURUS'S* FOSSILS WERE FIRST DISCOVERED, SCIENTISTS THOUGHT THEY BELONGED TO A GIANT TURTLE.

24 THE MEAT-EATING *DAKOTARAPTOR* HAD A KILLER CLAW 24 CM (9 IN) LONG.

WHICH DINOSAUR HAD THE
LONGEST CLAWS?

Dinosaur claws can reveal a lot about how these incredible creatures lived. While plant-eaters had short nails or hooves that protected their fingers and toes, most meat-eaters were armed with deadly hand and toe claws. These predatory dinosaurs used them like hooks, seizing their victim before taking chunks out of them. But one unusual theropod, *Therizinosaurus*, was a plant-eater. It used its colossal scythe-like claws for stripping leaves.

One of the claws was longer than the others.

FAST FACTS

Fossil of an *Apatosaurus* thumb claw

The massive herbivore *Apatosaurus* had a large thumb claw on the first digit of each hand. The bony claw was about 30 cm (12 in) long and may have been used for digging a hole for its eggs.

Each hand claw was as long as a banana.

Deinocheirus, a close cousin of *Therizinosaurus*, lived about 70 MYA. It had the longest arms of any known theropod — up to 2.4 m (8 ft) long — and large three-fingered hands with blunt claws, which it used to tear tough vegetation.

The claw had a sharp tip.

Unlike other theropods, *Baryonyx* hunted prey both on land and in the water. It may have used its curved thumb claw to hook fish out of the water — fossils of *Baryonyx* have been found with fish remains as well as the bones of a baby dinosaur.

Cats have retractable claws – to keep them sharp they are withdrawn when not hunting or climbing trees.

KERATIN IS A PROTEIN – THE SAME MATERIAL FORMS FEATHERS, HORNS, FINGERNAILS, AND THE HAIR ON YOUR HEAD.

SMALLER BIRD-LIKE HUNTERS SUCH AS *VELOCIRAPTOR* MAY HAVE USED THEIR CLAWS TO CLIMB TREES.

PLANT-EATERS

With its long neck, rotund body, and gigantic claws *Therizinosaurus* was a strange-looking dinosaur. As the first fossils were incomplete and so known only from a handful of bones, scientists could not agree on what type of animal *Therizinosaurus* was. However, we now know that *Therizinosaurus* was a type of theropod, the same group of dinosaurs that includes such ferocious meat-eaters as *Tyrannosaurus* and *Velociraptor*, but *Therizinosaurus* ate plants.

Therizinosaurus was the **largest** of the maniraptorans, a group of long-armed theropods.

HOW DID
DINOSAURS HUNT?

The meat-eating dinosaurs ranged in size from small bird-like creatures to fearsome giants like *Tyrannosaurus*. They all ran on two feet, using their speed to outrun their fleeing prey and then seizing it with their claws or teeth. Most of them probably targeted victims smaller than themselves, but a few were equipped to deal with the supersized plant-eaters of their era. Some may even have ganged up to attack the same large animal, and overwhelm it by sheer weight of numbers.

The hunter's heavy tail helped it keep its balance.

Allosaurus was more than 8.5 m (28 ft) long and weighed well over 2 tonnes (2.2 tons).

FAST FACTS

Very small hunters like the chicken-sized *Shuvuuia* would have preyed on insects, lizards, and small mammals. *Shuvuuia* had short but strong arms that it probably used to dig burrowing prey out of the ground. It almost certainly hunted at night.

MANY DINOSAURS BROKE TEETH WHEN ATTACKING PREY, BUT UNLIKE US THEY WERE ALWAYS ABLE TO GROW NEW ONES.

SCIENTISTS CAN WORK OUT HOW PREDATORY DINOSAURS HUNTED FROM THEIR TEETH, CLAWS, AND EVEN THEIR FOSSILIZED STOMACH CONTENTS.

SPECIAL TACTICS

Velociraptor and its close relatives, such as the bigger *Deinonychus*, were equipped with a hooked, extra-sharp claw on each foot. They may have used this to pin prey to the ground while ripping it apart with their teeth. Modern eagles use a similar technique.

This hooked claw was raised off ground to keep it sharp.

Deinonychus

Tyrannosaurus had tiny arms that would not have been of much use when hunting. It probably charged into the attack, relying on its massive jaws to cripple big prey — the deadly tactic used today by the great white shark.

Stout teeth did not shatter when they struck bone.

Tyrannosaurus

Stegosaurus could defend itself with its spiked tail.

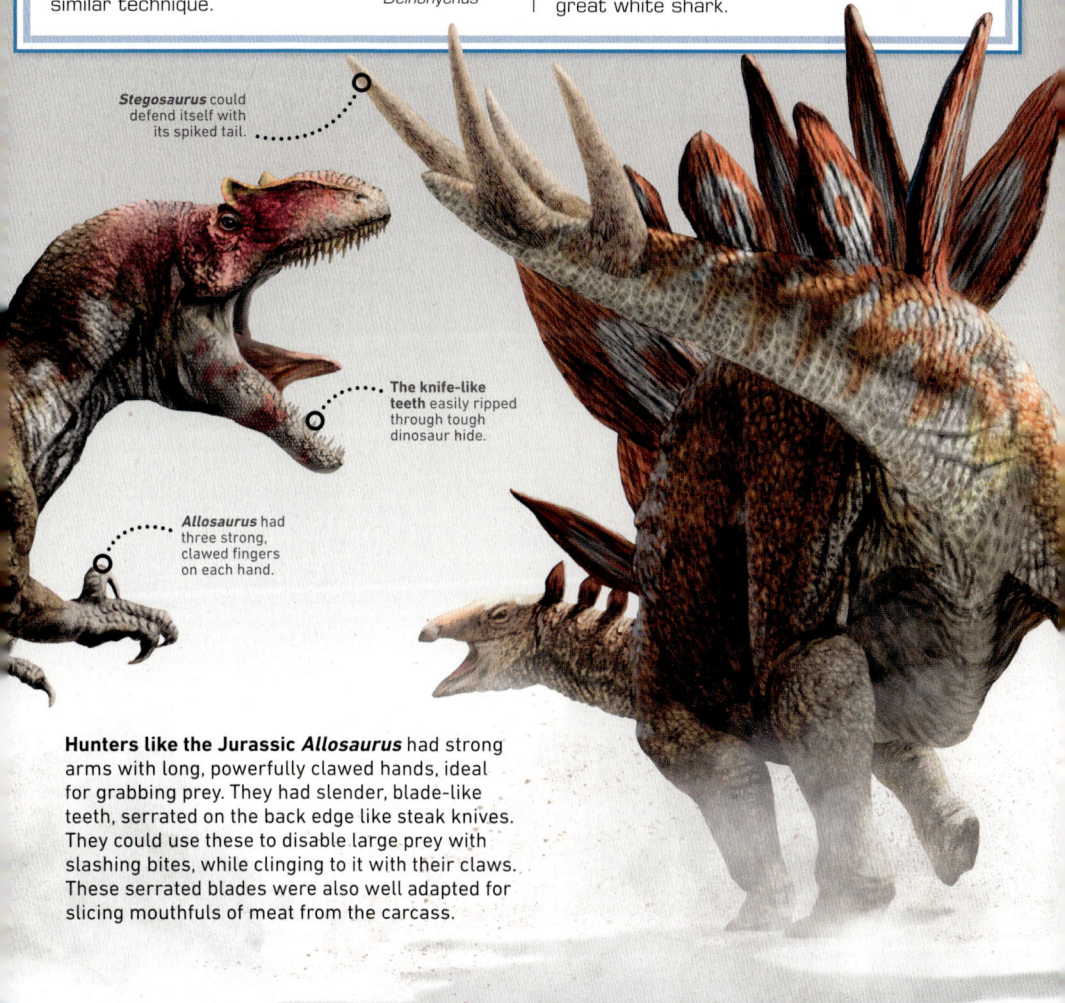

The knife-like teeth easily ripped through tough dinosaur hide.

Allosaurus had three strong, clawed fingers on each hand.

Hunters like the Jurassic *Allosaurus* had strong arms with long, powerfully clawed hands, ideal for grabbing prey. They had slender, blade-like teeth, serrated on the back edge like steak knives. They could use these to disable large prey with slashing bites, while clinging to it with their claws. These serrated blades were also well adapted for slicing mouthfuls of meat from the carcass.

THE CHEETAH – THE FASTEST LAND ANIMAL ON EARTH – RELIES ON ITS SPEED TO CHASE DOWN PREY.

ANALYSIS OF THEIR BRAINS SHOWS THAT HUNTING DINOSAURS HAD VERY SHARP SENSES, LIKE MODERN EAGLES AND OWLS.

WHICH DINOSAUR HAD THE
TOUGHEST ARMOUR?

Some of the toughest dinosaurs to have ever lived were part of a family of plant-eating dinosaurs called ankylosaurs. Built like tanks, they were armed with spikes, bony plates, and clubbed tails. One of the largest of all the ankylosaurs was *Ankylosaurus*. It used its strong armour to defend itself in a habitat full of fierce meat-eating predators like *Tyrannosaurus rex*.

The tough, leathery skin was studded with rows of bony plates called osteoderms.

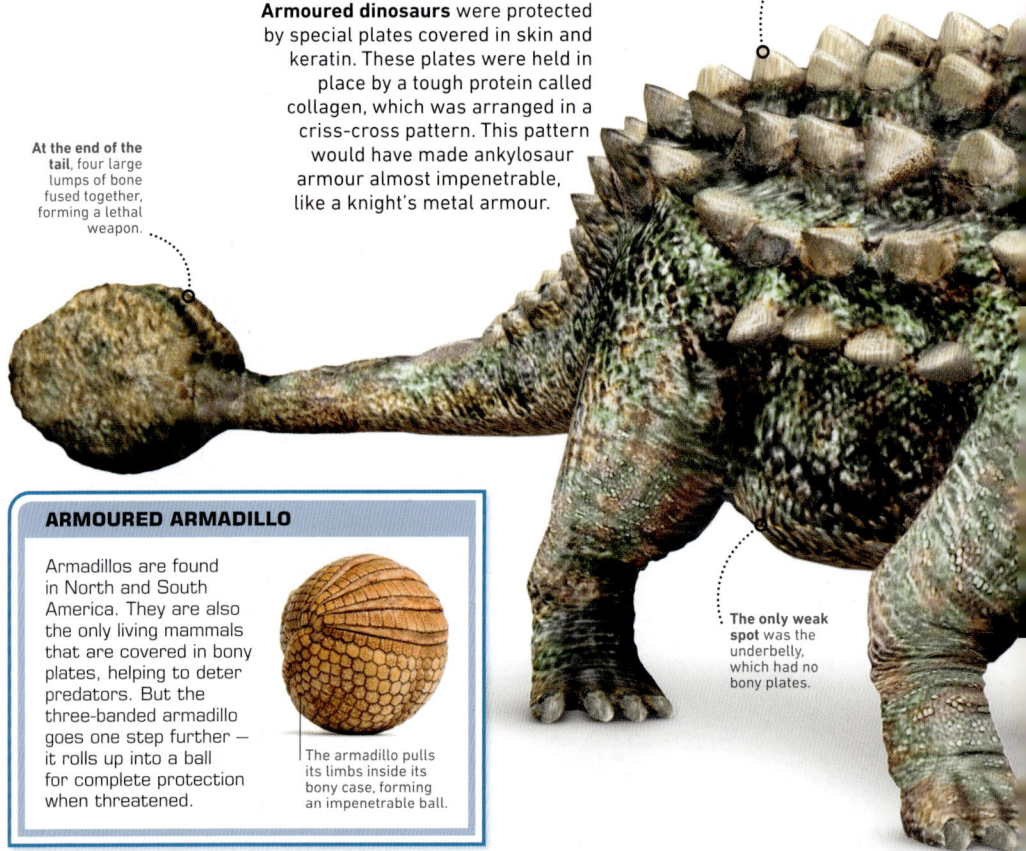

Armoured dinosaurs were protected by special plates covered in skin and keratin. These plates were held in place by a tough protein called collagen, which was arranged in a criss-cross pattern. This pattern would have made ankylosaur armour almost impenetrable, like a knight's metal armour.

At the end of the tail, four large lumps of bone fused together, forming a lethal weapon.

The only weak spot was the underbelly, which had no bony plates.

ARMOURED ARMADILLO

Armadillos are found in North and South America. They are also the only living mammals that are covered in bony plates, helping to deter predators. But the three-banded armadillo goes one step further — it rolls up into a ball for complete protection when threatened.

The armadillo pulls its limbs inside its bony case, forming an impenetrable ball.

AN *ANKYLOSAURUS'S* ARMOUR ALONE WOULD HAVE WEIGHED AS MUCH AS A BLACK RHINOCEROS.

THE BONY PLATES OF AN *ANKYLOSAURUS* RANGED FROM THE SIZE OF A SMALL COIN TO THE SIZE OF A BASKETBALL.

FAST FACTS

The fossils of one of the smallest ankylosaurs, *Minmi*, were discovered in Australia in 1964. This Cretaceous dinosaur had small bony plates on its underbelly as well as extra bones on its back, which may have helped support its muscles.

Fossil evidence shows that *Minmi* was about 3 m (10 ft) long.

One of the world's best preserved dinosaur fossil was discovered in Canada in 2011. The 110-million-year-old fossil of an armoured dinosaur named *Borealopelta* is so well preserved that it looks like a 3-D replica of a sleeping dinosaur.

Borealopelta's bony spikes

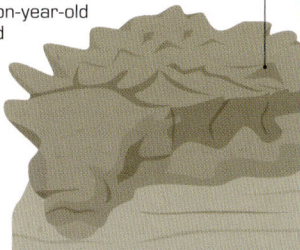

The head was covered with small interlocking bony plates, shielding the dinosaur from the deadly jaws of predators.

Knights wore tough, heavy armour to protect them from enemy weapons.

Long spikes jutted out from the back of the head and from the sides of the face.

Ankylosaurus's armour was **tough** enough to withstand the bite of a *T. rex*.

THE FIRST DINOSAUR FOSSIL FOUND IN ANTARCTICA WAS OF AN ANKYLOSAUR CALLED *ANTARCTOPELTA*.

BOREALOPELTA WAS ABOUT AS LONG AS AN AMERICAN CROCODILE.

LASHING OUT

Even for a superpredator like *Tyrannosaurus*, an *Ankylosaurus* was a tough nut to crack. Its massively thick plates of armour may have been strong enough to break the killer's teeth, and it could lash out with a weapon of its own — its heavy clubbed tail. Swung like a sledgehammer, this could inflict crippling injuries, possibly even breaking a leg. Perhaps even *Tyrannosaurus* soon learned to leave it alone and choose softer targets.

For added strength, an *Ankylosaurus*'s skull bones were fused together.

LETHAL WEAPON

The terrifying hunter *Allosaurus* lived at the same time as *Alcovasaurus* and *Stegasaurus*. It would have tried to ambush the plant-eating stegasaurs, then bash them with its spiky tail — an *Allosaurus* bone has been found with a hole from the spike of a *Stegasaurus*.

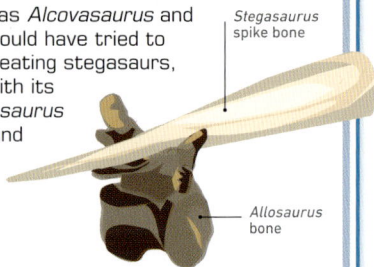

Stegasaurus spike bone

Allosaurus bone

Alcovasaurus's **tail spikes** measured 1 m (3 ft) in length.

These long tail spikes may also have been used to slash through vegetation.

WHICH DINOSAUR HAD THE
LONGEST ARMOUR SPIKES?

With two rows of massive bony plates running down its back and long spikes at the end of its tail, *Stegosaurus* is one of the most easily recognizable dinosaurs. But there is one dinosaur that may have had even longer spikes at the end of its tail – *Alcovasaurus*, a close relative of *Stegosaurus*. *Alcovasaurus* was an elephant-sized plant-eater with a spiky, flexible tail – an effective defensive weapon, allowing the dinosaur to lash out at its predators.

2016

IT WAS NOT UNTIL 2016 THAT *ALCOVASAURUS* WAS IDENTIFIED AS A **NEW SPECIES**.

THE SPIKE-TAILED *KENTROSAURUS* MAY HAVE BEEN ABLE TO SWING ITS TAIL AT A TOP SPEED OF 145 KPH (90 MPH).

FAST FACTS

Some modern-day animals are covered in spikes, spines, or quills. These are modified hairs that are both stiff and strong. A hedgehog has up to 7,000 sharp spines, which it uses as defence.

A hedgehog rolls into a prickly ball when threatened.

Despite its threatening appearance the thorny devil from the deserts of Australia is completely harmless. To defend itself from predators, it has an armour of sharp spikes, making it too prickly to eat.

The small lizard is covered from head to tail in thorn-like spikes.

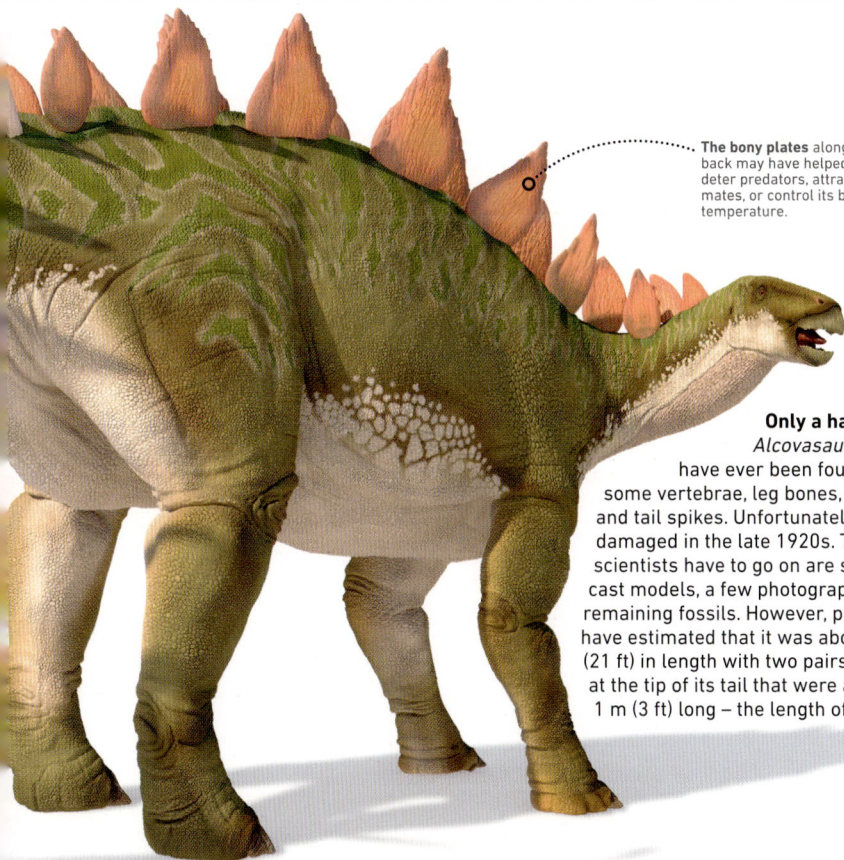

The bony plates along its back may have helped to deter predators, attract mates, or control its body temperature.

Only a handful of *Alcovasaurus* fossils have ever been found, including some vertebrae, leg bones, several ribs, and tail spikes. Unfortunately, these were damaged in the late 1920s. Today, all scientists have to go on are some plaster cast models, a few photographs, and some remaining fossils. However, palaeontologists have estimated that it was about 6.5 m (21 ft) in length with two pairs of spikes at the tip of its tail that were at least 1 m (3 ft) long – the length of a guitar.

25
ALCOVASAURUS HAD A TAIL THAT WAS 25% SHORTER THAN A *STEGOSAURUS*, BUT ITS TAIL SPIKES WERE TWICE AS LONG.

GIGANTSPINOSAURUS HAD HUGE SPIKES ON ITS SHOULDERS MEASURING 0.6 M (2 FT) IN LENGTH.

Most of the brain's bulk was devoted to controlling the animal's enormous body.

The brain occupied a cavity at the back of the skull.

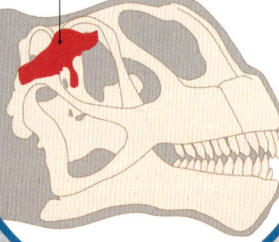

Sauropods had huge bodies but tiny heads that housed a very small brain.

Sauropod dinosaurs like *Camarasaurus* were the biggest land animals that ever lived, yet they had very small skulls and brain cavities. The brain did not even fill the entire cavity. The part devoted to the sense of smell was relatively big, so this must have been vital to their survival.

HOW BIG WERE
DINOSAUR BRAINS?

Some dinosaurs had astonishingly small brains compared to their bodies. The gigantic sauropod *Camarasaurus* could grow 23 m (75 ft) long, yet its brain was no heavier than a lemon. Clearly it was all the animal needed – possibly because it was a plant-eater with few problems to solve. Hunters like the small theropod *Stenonychosaurus* needed to outwit their prey, so it makes sense that their brains were relatively much bigger. Even so, it is unlikely that they were smarter than the average chicken.

SCIENTISTS USE **X-RAY SCANNING** TO SEE INSIDE DINOSAUR SKULLS AND CREATE IMAGES OF THEIR BRAINS.

RELATIVE TO ITS BODY, A **MOUSE'S BRAIN** IS THE SAME SIZE AS A HUMAN'S, SO BRAIN SIZE MAY NOT BE THE BEST INDICATOR OF INTELLIGENCE.

Meat-eating dinosaurs had larger brains than plant-eaters. The biggest found so far, compared to body weight, is that of *Stenonychosaurus* – an agile, lightweight hunter about 2.4 m (8 ft) long. Its brain was still surprisingly small, but more of its bulk would have been devoted to memory and problem-solving.

The relative brain size was similar to that of modern birds.

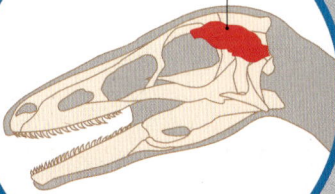

Catching prey takes cunning as well as sharp senses and quick reactions.

FAST FACTS

Birds are descended from theropod dinosaurs — and some, such as crows, are very intelligent. Their brains contain a lot of densely packed cells, so they are smarter than their brain size would suggest. Could the same apply to some extinct dinosaurs?

New Caledonian crow

If mud fills the inside of a dead dinosaur's brain cavity, it can harden to form a cast of its brain. Scientists can mimic this process by using liquid rubber. This cast of a *Tyrannosaurus* brain shows that it was unlike a human brain, but similar in shape to a crocodile's brain.

The brain cast is about the size of a banana.

In 2004, a fossil hunter in England found a fragment of fossilized brain tissue inside the broken skull of a big plant-eating dinosaur similar to *Iguanodon*. The structure of the fossil brain shows similarities with the brains of birds and crocodiles, which are the nearest surviving relatives of extinct dinosaurs.

Iguanodon roamed Europe more than 125 MYA.

Iguanodon

THE **NEW CALEDONIAN CROW** IS ONE OF THE FEW ANIMALS THAT CAN MAKE AND USE TOOLS.

A **HUMAN BRAIN** LOOKS DIFFERENT FROM A DINOSAUR BRAIN BECAUSE OF ITS HUGE CEREBRUM — THE PART USED FOR THINKING.

FAST FACTS

Many birds can sing, thanks to an organ called the syrinx. This has two branches that work separately, allowing a bird to make two sounds at once. Since birds are descended from theropod dinosaurs, some of these may have had similar vocal skills.

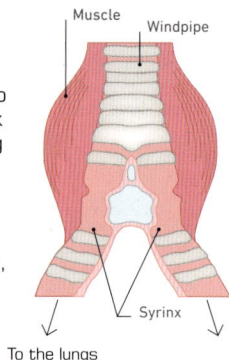

Muscle

Windpipe

Syrinx

To the lungs

Alligators — and crocodiles — are relatives of dinosaurs. They can grunt, growl, and bellow. But they can also produce a deep rumbling sound. This "infrasound" is too low-pitched for us to hear, but the vibrations travel through the ground or water. Elephants can make similar sounds.

The vibrations make the water "dance" off its back.

Some modern animals, including several frogs, seals, and apes, have inflatable vocal sacs that make their calls much louder. The plant-eating dinosaur *Muttaburrasaurus* had a hollow structure on its snout that might have supported a similar vocal sac.

The vocal sac might have inflated like a balloon.

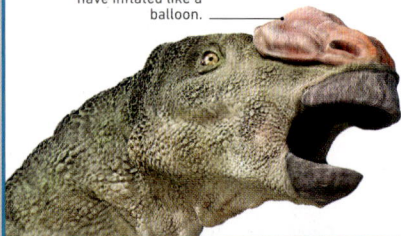

DID DINOSAURS
ROAR?

Nearly all living land animals use sound to communicate with each other, and extinct dinosaurs were probably just as vocal. Some of their fossils have features that seem to be connected with making noises of a kind. Modern birds – which inherited much of their anatomy from dinosaur ancestors – certainly have. Depending on their nature, dinosaurs may have grunted, trumpeted, whistled, squeaked, or even rumbled – but so far scientists have no evidence that any of them could roar.

Parasaurolophus reached lengths of up to 9.5 m (30 ft), and weighed about 2.5 tonnes (3 tons).

DINOSAURS WOULD HAVE USED SOUND TO KEEP IN TOUCH, ATTRACT MATES, AND WARN OF DANGER.

TYRANNOSAURUS MAY HAVE MADE RUMBLING CALLS LIKE THOSE OF ALLIGATORS AND ELEPHANTS.

The 1-m (3-ft) long crest had a bony core that was covered by skin.

Air passed through the crest.

Nostrils

The very long crest of *Parasaurolophus* contained tubes leading from the nostrils to the end of the crest and back. Related species had tubes of different lengths, so they probably sounded different too.

We know that one group of dinosaurs almost certainly made noises. *Parasaurolophus* and its relatives had skulls with big, bony crests containing air passages linked to their nostrils. These may have acted as megaphones to make their calls louder. It is likely that these dinosaurs lived in forests, where calling to each other helped them stay in contact when they were hidden among the trees.

NATURAL TRUMPET

An elephant's trunk is an extension of its windpipe, which contains its larynx (voice box). This enables it to make loud trumpeting calls that travel long distances. *Parasaurolophus* may have used the air passages in its crest to make the same kinds of penetrating sounds.

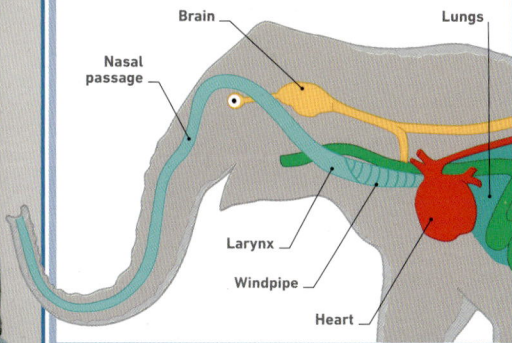

Brain

Lungs

Nasal passage

Larynx

Windpipe

Heart

SO FAR, NO SYRINX HAS BEEN FOUND IN A DINOSAUR FOSSIL SO THEY PROBABLY COULD NOT SING.

THE DEEP RUMBLING CALLS MADE BY ELEPHANTS CAN BE DETECTED FROM 10 KM (6 MILES) AWAY.

BROWSING GIANTS

A typical sauropod had a very long, flexible, muscular neck, balanced by a long tail. This enabled it to stand still and feed over a wide area, on the ground and high in the trees. Its teeth and jaws were adapted to gather large amounts of leafy food very quickly, so it had no difficulty satisfying its enormous appetite.

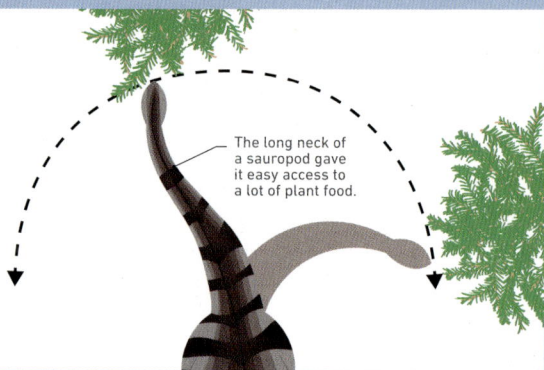

The long neck of a sauropod gave it easy access to a lot of plant food.

The largest living land animal is the African bush elephant. But the mighty Jurassic sauropod *Apatosaurus* would have weighed more than three times as much, and some titanosaurs were even bigger. Today's largest living animal, the blue whale, is supported by the water, while a sauropod had to stand on its own four feet. What was the point of being so big? Certainly their huge size deterred their enemies. But mostly a huge body could carry a big digestive system that could process vast quantities of vegetation and turn it into yet more dinosaur flesh.

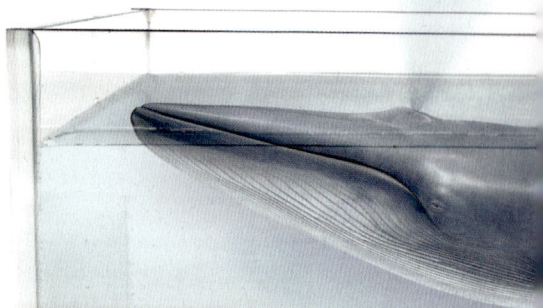

The huge sauropod *Apatosaurus* could have weighed more than 33 tonnes (36 tons).

The pillar-like legs supported the dinosaur's weight.

A big African bush elephant can weigh 10 tonnes (11 tons).

THE COLOSSAL SAUROPOD *ARGENTINOSAURUS* WAS ABOUT 35 M (115 FT) LONG AND MAY HAVE WEIGHED 75 TONNES (83 TONS).

THE SMALLEST KNOWN SAUROPOD, *MAGYAROSAURUS*, GREW TO LENGTHS OF ABOUT 6 M (20 FT).

HOW DID SAUROPODS
GET SO BIG?

The biggest land animals that ever existed were sauropods – giant, long-necked, plant-eating dinosaurs that walked on four huge, pillar-like legs. Many were far bigger than any animal alive today, especially some of the aptly named titanosaurs that lived towards the end of the dinosaur era. But why did they grow so big, and how did they gather enough food to fuel their massive bodies? We are still not sure, but their fossil remains have given us some clues.

FAST FACTS

The colossal squid is a giant of the deep. The largest of all invertebrates (animals without backbones), it can reach lengths of up to 14 m (46 ft) and weigh more than 500 kg (1,100 lb).

At 12 m (40 ft) long, the whale shark is the biggest fish in the world. It weighs about 18 tonnes (20 tons).

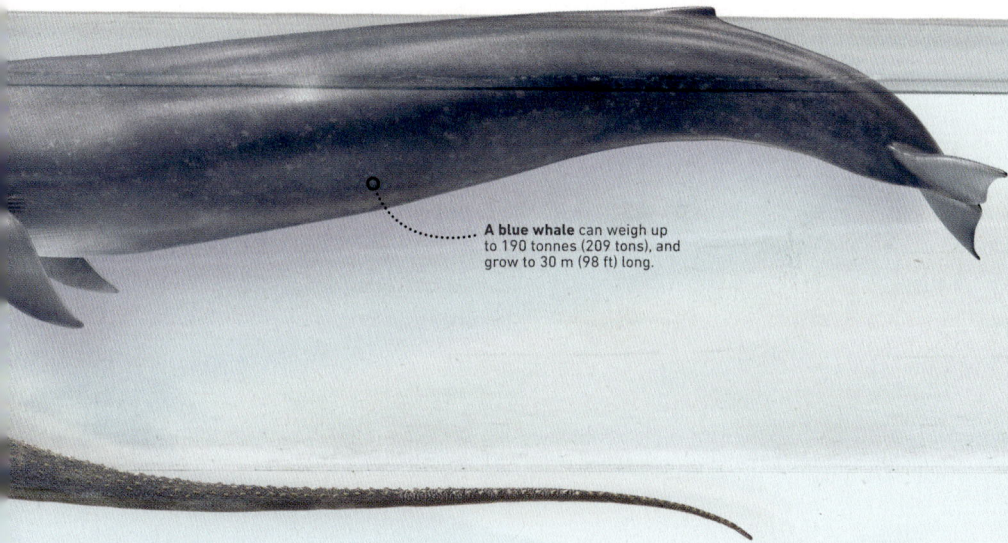

A blue whale can weigh up to 190 tonnes (209 tons), and grow to 30 m (98 ft) long.

TO WORK OUT A DINOSAUR'S WEIGHT, SCIENTISTS CREATE 3-D COMPUTER MODELS.

AS WELL AS BEING THE LARGEST, THE AFRICAN BUSH ELEPHANT IS ALSO THE HEAVIEST LAND ANIMAL.

HOW BIG WERE
DINOSAUR EGGS?

As far as we know, all dinosaurs laid eggs. They had hard shells like birds' eggs, but were mostly a different shape. Depending on the type of dinosaur that laid them, some were round like balls, while others were long ovals. Many were laid in nests, similar to those of modern birds. Other eggs have been found buried in the ground and may have been covered by leaves that warmed up as they decayed. As for their size, they could be very big – but not as big as we might expect!

BABY YINGLIANG

Most dinosaur eggs hatched, but a few have been found intact with unhatched babies still inside them. This one, found in China in 2000, contained the fossilized bones of a bird-like oviraptorosaur that has been called Baby Yingliang.

Dinosaur embryo fossil

Baby Yingliang was tucked inside its egg, similar to modern bird embryos when they are about to hatch.

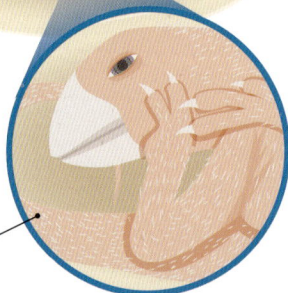

Dinosaur eggs were surprisingly small. They look big compared to birds' eggs, but many were tiny compared to the huge animals that produced them. The gigantic, long-necked sauropod *Apatosaurus* could grow to a length of 30 m (98 ft) or more, but its ball-shaped eggs were just 30 cm (12 in) across. This means that its babies were very small, and must have grown up fast. The largest known extinct dinosaur eggs were laid by theropods, belonging to a group called caenagnathids.

Citipati, a bird-like theropod dinosaur, laid clutches of long, narrow eggs.

Chicken egg
5 cm (2 in) long

Citipati egg
18 cm (7 in) long

IN 1923, AN EXPEDITION TO MONGOLIA DISCOVERED THE **FIRST** FOSSIL DINOSAUR EGGS.

THE **SMALLEST** FOSSIL DINOSAUR EGG FOUND SO FAR IS SMALLER THAN A GOLF BALL.

FAST FACTS

Some dinosaurs nested in colonies. One colony discovered in 1997 near Auca Mahuevo, Argentina, contains thousands of eggs that were laid 80 MYA.

The ground is littered with egg fragments.

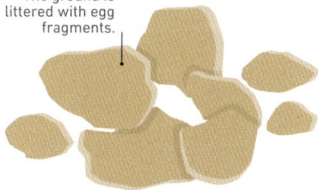

The **largest** known dinosaur eggs were 60 cm (24 in) long and about 20 cm (8 in) wide.

Apatosaurus, a giant sauropod, laid round eggs the size of watermelons.

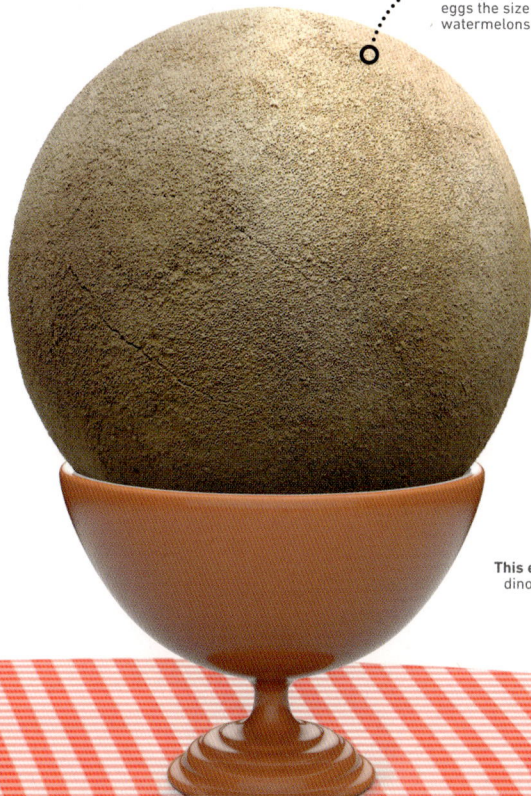

This egg was laid by a dinosaur resembling a giant ostrich.

Apatosaurus egg
30 cm (12 in) across

Caenagnathid egg
60 cm (24 in) long

IN 1976, DINOSAUR EGGS WERE DISCOVERED IN SOUTH AFRICA. LAID ABOUT 190 MYA, THEY ARE THE OLDEST KNOWN FOSSIL EGGS.

THE EXTINCT ELEPHANT BIRD OF MADAGASCAR LAID EGGS BIGGER THAN THOSE OF THE BIGGEST GIANT DINOSAURS.

HOW FAST DID BABY
DINOSAURS GROW?

The largest dinosaurs were gigantic animals. An adult sauropod –
one of the long-necked plant-eaters – could weigh more than six
African elephants. But a sauropod egg was no bigger than a football,
and the baby that hatched from it was barely the size of a newborn
human baby, with a weight of about 4 kg (9 lb). In 30 years, the
dinosaur hatchling could become an adult weighing perhaps
10,000 times as much. This means that it grew at a phenomenal
rate, gaining up to 1,800 kg (4,000 lb) a year – far more than any
other land animal, living or extinct.

FAST FACTS

Although young dinosaurs grew at an astonishing rate, they took a surprisingly long time to hatch. Analysis of unhatched dinosaur babies shows that some stayed in the egg for up to six months.

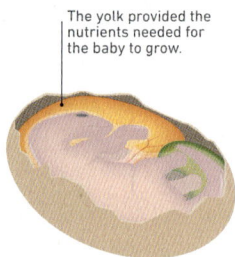

The yolk provided the nutrients needed for the baby to grow.

The fossil skeletons of young dinosaurs show that, like most young animals, including this baby gorilla, they had oversized heads and feet. As they grew, their body size gradually caught up, until they gained adult proportions.

Newborn gorilla

In 2000, the fossil bones of a young *Rapetosaurus*
were found in a museum collection. This was a
titanosaur – a type of sauropod that, when adult,
weighed more than two African elephants. The
young *Rapetosaurus* was about two months old
when it died. It would have stood 35 cm (14 in) at
the hip – as big as a golden retriever – and weighed
40 kg (88 lb). But when newly hatched it would
have weighed about ten times less, showing just
how fast a dinosaur could grow.

The baby that hatched from an egg of this size would have weighed around 4 kg (9 lb).

The biggest sauropod egg found so far was the size of a football, and most were smaller at about 12 cm (5 in) across.

**THE FOSSILS OF THE
YOUNG *RAPETOSAURUS*
ARE THE MOST
COMPLETE OF ANY
YOUNG TITANOSAUR.**

**BABY *MAIASAURA*
STAYED IN OR NEAR THE
NEST FOR UP TO A YEAR
WHILE THEIR PARENTS
BROUGHT THEM FOOD.**

GROWING UP

Different types of dinosaur seem to have grown to full adult size at different rates. A *Tyrannosaurus* was fully grown at 20 years old, but a *Maiasaura* — a plant-eating hadrosaur up to 9 m (30 ft) long — reached full size at eight. When newly hatched, a baby *Maiasaura* was 40 cm (16 in) long, but it grew to 1.5 m (5 ft) long within its first year.

Maiasaura family

At 15 m (50 ft) long, *Rapetosaurus* was twice the length of a bus.

A golden retriever takes between 16 and 24 months to reach full size.

The young *Rapetosaurus* would have been tiny compared to its parents.

TYRANNOSAURUS HAD A GROWTH SPURT BETWEEN THE AGES OF 15 AND 20 – IT PUT ON MORE THAN 2 KG (4 LB) PER DAY.

SCIENTISTS FIRST OBSERVED THE GROWTH LINES IN DINOSAUR BONES WHEN STUDYING THE FOSSILS OF A JURASSIC SAUROPOD IN 1981.

Brachiosaurus roamed the forests of North America and may have lived in herds for safety.

DINOSAUR BABIES

Dinosaurs were a diverse group of animals, and different types would have looked after their young in different ways. We know that some, like *Maiasaura*, tended their young in the nest, supplying food and driving away predators. Others, like the long-necked sauropod *Brachiosaurus*, may have encouraged their young to tag along as they moved away from the nest site to find food. Some tracks of fossil footprints suggest that young dinosaurs often travelled with older ones like this.

HOW LONG DID
DINOSAURS LIVE?

Scientists once thought that giant dinosaurs grew at the same slow rate as lizards, crocodiles, and other modern reptiles. If so, they must have lived for several hundred years to get so big! But it is now clear that dinosaurs grew far more quickly, enabling some to reach truly colossal size within lifespans very similar to our own. Analysis of their fossil remains backs this up, revealing that gigantic dinosaurs like *Tyrannosaurus* were just a few decades old when they died.

Huge sauropods like *Diplodocus* could probably live for about 80 years.

30

TRIX, THE OLDEST SPECIMEN OF *TYRANNOSAURUS* FOUND SO FAR, WAS ABOUT **30 YEARS OLD** WHEN SHE DIED.

JUDGING BY THE **LIFESPANS** OF MODERN ANIMALS, SMALL DINOSAURS PROBABLY DID NOT LIVE AS LONG AS GIANT ONES.

FAST FACTS

Some insects have very short lives. Adult mayflies live for only a few hours after hatching — just long enough for them to mate and lay their eggs.

A few animals can live for centuries. Some of the giant barrel sponges that live on the bed of the Caribbean Sea are estimated to be at least 2,300 years old.

In 1983, scientists studying the bones of *Bothriospondylus*, a big plant-eating sauropod, discovered that it had died at the age of 43. But the animal was only half grown, so it must have died while still relatively young. To reach full size it would have had to live for another 30 years or more, giving it a potential lifespan of 80 years. Big meat-eating theropods probably had shorter lives of up to 30 years.

GROWTH RINGS

As a bone grows, new material is added to the outside. In seasonal climates this happens at different rates, creating thicker and thinner layers. If a dinosaur bone is sawn in half, the layers can show up as annual growth rings, revealing the animal's age when it died.

This cross-section of a dinosaur bone shows its growth rings.

THE OLDEST KNOWN LAND ANIMAL WAS AN ALDABRA GIANT TORTOISE THAT DIED IN 2006 AT AN ESTIMATED AGE OF 255.

TREES CAN REACH INCREDIBLE AGES. SOME AMERICAN BRISTLECONE PINES ARE MORE THAN 5,000 YEARS OLD.

Inside out

LAST MEAL

About 110 MYA, an armoured dinosaur named *Borealopelta* feasted on plants in what is now Alberta, Canada. In 2011, a miner discovered its remains, which included its stomach contents. **These showed what it had been eating — 24 types of plant, especially ferns. Some of the leaves had traces of charcoal, suggesting they had grown after a forest fire.**

STOMACH STONES

Some plant-eating dinosaurs swallowed stones to help their muscular stomachs grind food to a digestible pulp. Modern crocodiles and some birds do the same. **Eventually, the stones become smooth and polished, which is how they can be identified among fossils.**

SUPER SENSES

These dinosaurs had some of the best senses in the prehistoric world.

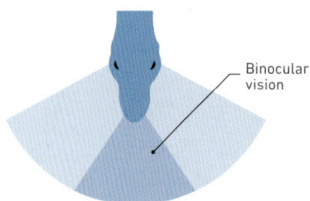

Binocular vision

▲ Huge peepers

Tyrannosaurus had super-sized eyes — each was about the size of an orange. They faced mainly forward, giving it **excellent binocular vision** for judging its deadly attacks. It could also see in great detail, enabling it to target prey from up to 6 km (4 miles) away.

▲ Best hearing

The bird-like dinosaur *Shuvuuia* had such **good hearing and vision**, it could hunt in complete darkness just like a modern-day owl. When analysing its skull anatomy, scientists discovered the structure responsible for hearing was much bigger than in other dinosaurs.

▲ Super sniffers

Theropods, including *Tyrannosaurus* and *Velociraptor* had an **acute sense of smell**. CT scans of *Tyrannosaurus's* skull show that the size of its olfactory bulb, the part of the brain that is responsible for identifying smells, was much larger in relation to its brain size.

MANY PLANT-EATERS SUPPORTED THEIR WEIGHT ON ALL FOUR LIMBS. THEY HAD STRONG FRONT LIMB AND SHOULDER BONES WITH HUGE MUSCLES.

MOST OF THE BIG DINOSAURS WERE PROTECTED BY SCALES, WHICH WERE MADE OF TOUGH KERATIN.

GROWING *UP*

Like humans, some dinosaurs learned to walk on four legs before transitioning to two legs when they were older. **Weighing just 450g** (16 oz) when it was born, *Mussaurus* probably walked on four legs when it first hatched, moving to two when its tail became big enough to allow it to balance on two legs.

STANDING TALL

▲ Upright stance

Like birds, dinosaurs stood with their legs directly under their bodies, which helped to support their weight. This upright stance also enabled dinosaurs to **run faster and for longer** than reptiles today.

▲ Sprawling stance

Some reptiles like lizards have limbs that stick out sideways. With their bellies often **touching the ground**, they are not efficient movers and their sprawling limbs do not support their weight.

▲ High walk stance

Unlike lizards, crocodiles can lift their body off the ground so that they can stand slightly more upright. They use this **"high walk"** when they want to move fast.

DINOSAUR *DISEASES*

From colds to aches and pains, dinosaurs weren't immune to some of the illnesses humans face today.

▶ Sniffles

In 2022, palaeontologists found evidence of a **dinosaur with a bad cold**. The young sauropod called Dolly had a respiratory infection, which caused abnormal bone growth on several of its neck bones. The infection probably would have caused **sneezing, fever, and coughing fits**.

▶ Toothache

Chomping down on plants and ripping into tough meat takes a toll on any animal's teeth, including those of dinosaurs. Some scientists think that Sue, the most complete *Tyrannosaurus* skeleton ever found, may have had an **awful toothache** due to three strange-looking teeth.

▶ Arthritis

About 70 MYA, a plant-eating duckbilled dinosaur had a **very painful arm**. Scientists found that it had **septic arthritis**, which is a bone disease that develops when an injury becomes infected.

MANY OF THE SMALLER THEROPODS WERE COVERED IN FEATHERS, HELPING TO KEEP THEM WARM, AND SOME WERE ABLE TO FLY.

SCIENTISTS DON'T KNOW A LOT ABOUT DINOSAUR BOTTOMS, BUT THEY THINK THEY LOOKED LIKE A CROCODILE'S, WITH ONE OPENING CALLED A CLOACA.

Curious creatures

Over the 550 million years that animals have existed on Earth, evolution has created a dazzling variety of strange creatures. Many that lived in the distant past were quite unlike the animals that live around us today.

One of the earliest animals to evolve, in Cambrian seas more than 500 MYA, *Hallucigenia* was also one of the most peculiar. Its fossils are so puzzling that, at first, scientists mistook its spines for its legs.

HOW BIG WERE PREHISTORIC CREEPY CRAWLIES?

Arthropleura was the size of a **small car**.

During the Carboniferous Period, more than 300 MYA, vast forests spread across the land and animals ventured far and wide. Oxygen levels were higher than today, and this is thought to be one of the key reasons why supersized creepy crawlies appeared. These ancient arthropods had tough external skeletons and jointed legs, like *Arthropleura*.

CAMBRIAN EXPLOSION

The beginning of the Cambrian Period, about 541 MYA, marked a significant step in the evolution of life on Earth. A major explosion of new lifeforms appeared, including many animals with hard parts, such as shells. Weird and wonderful creatures evolved like the bizarre, worm-like *Hallucigenia*. Fossils of this creature show that it was about 5 cm (2 in) long and had tiny needle-like teeth lining its throat as well as its mouth.

Hallucigenia had multiple rows of thin spikes on its back.

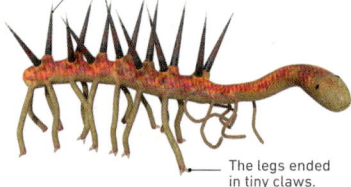

The legs ended in tiny claws.

Arthropleura was the largest land arthropod to have ever lived. Fossils suggest that it was about 55 cm (22 in) wide, up to 2.6 m (8.5 ft) long, and weighed about 50 kg (110 lb). Like modern millipedes, it grew larger by shedding its hard outer skeleton. Despite its intimidating appearance, *Arthropleura* was a herbivore.

SOME *ARTHROPLEURA* FOSSILS HAVE TRACES OF PLANT REMAINS INSIDE THE GUT.

50 TRACKS SHOW THAT AN *ARTHROPLEURA*'S LEGS WERE ABOUT 50 CM (20 IN) APART.

FOSSILS OF *ARTHROPLEURA* HAVE BEEN FOUND IN NORTH AMERICA AND EUROPE.

89

The body consisted of 30 jointed segments, which were covered by armoured plates.

FAST FACTS

Isotelus rex

Trilobites were ancient marine arthropods. The largest of them, *Isotelus rex*, which means the "king of trilobites", reached lengths of up to 70 cm (28 in), about the same size as an umbrella. They thrived in the oceans for more than 270 million years.

Arthropleura used its long antennae to sense and feel its way around the swampy forest floor.

Two pairs of legs were attached to each segment, making 120 legs in total.

INSECTS WERE THE FIRST ANIMALS TO FLY.

TODAY, THERE ARE ABOUT 1.4 BILLION INSECTS FOR EVERY PERSON ON EARTH.

AIRBORNE HUNTER

At the same time as the supersized millipede *Arthropleura* was scuttling over the ground, giant insects were swooping through the air. They included the griffinflies, relatives of dragonflies that hunted other insects. The fossils of one of these, *Meganeura*, show that it had a wingspan of about 70 cm (28 in) — more than four times the wingspan of the largest living dragonfly.

Meganeura hunted on the wing, seizing flying insects with its spiny legs.

HOW BIG WAS A
SEA SCORPION?

Sea scorpions are not true scorpions. They are an extinct group of prehistoric arthropods called eurypterids. The largest-known sea scorpion of all time was *Jaekelopterus*, which was larger than an adult human. *Jaekelopterus* lived more than 400 MYA, prowling the lakes and rivers of North America. It was the top predator in its environment, preying on trilobites and fish, and may even have feasted on other sea scorpions.

The pincer-like claws were used for seizing and tearing prey.

The four pairs of legs were used for walking on the seabed.

FAST FACTS

The first eurypterid fossil, *Eurypterus remipes*, was discovered in 1818 in New York, USA. Originally thought to be a catfish, it was correctly identified in 1825 as an ancient sea scorpion. It is now the state fossil of New York.

Fossil of *Eurypterus remipes*

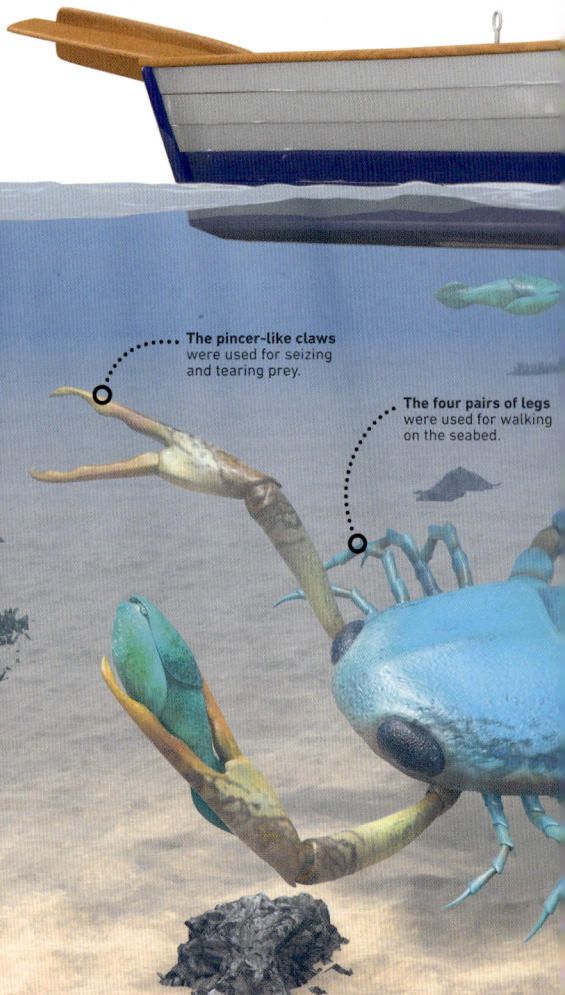

NOT ALL PREHISTORIC SEA SCORPIONS WERE BIG – SOME WERE ONLY THE SIZE OF YOUR HAND.

SEA SCORPIONS WENT EXTINCT AROUND 250 MYA – THE TIME OF THE PERMIAN MASS EXTINCTION.

SIZE CLUE

In 2007, palaeontologists described a gigantic *Jaekelopterus* claw found in Germany. It measured 46 cm (18 in) long. From this, scientists were able to work out the sea scorpion's body length – it was at least half a metre longer than previously estimated. It is very likely that it grew to this immense size as it did not have any predators, except for other large eurypterids. The biggest scorpions today are only about 20 cm (8 in) in length.

Jaekelopterus claw

Emperor scorpion

Reaching lengths of up to 2.6 m (9 ft), there was no getting away from this colossal creature. It was an active hunter with superb vision for spotting fast-moving prey and probably ambushed its dinner. It used its sharp claws (called chelicerae) to slice its prey into smaller, more edible pieces.

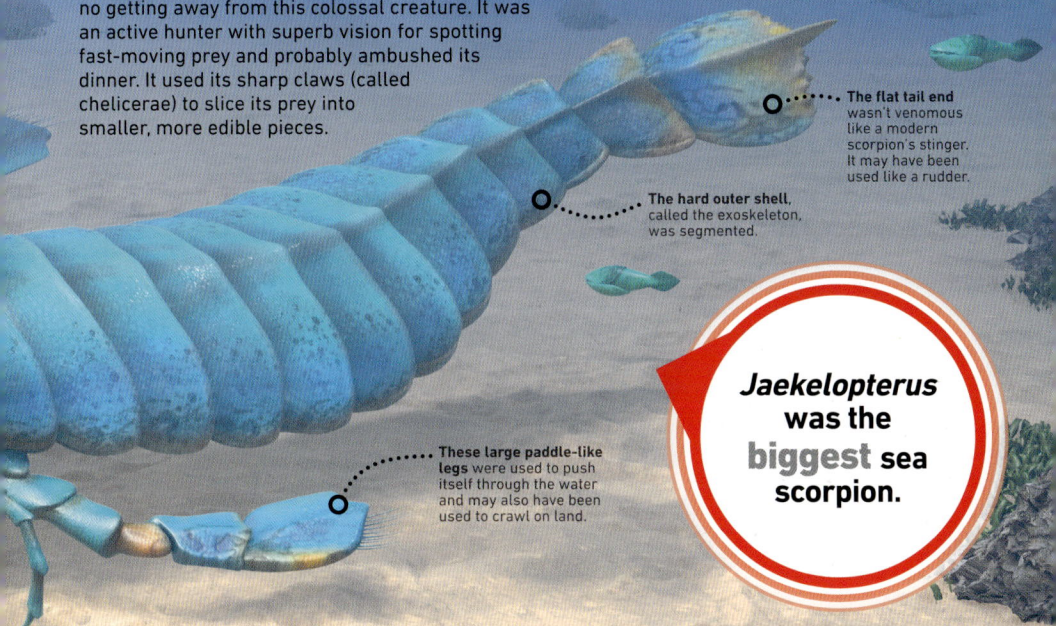

The flat tail end wasn't venomous like a modern scorpion's stinger. It may have been used like a rudder.

The hard outer shell, called the exoskeleton, was segmented.

These large paddle-like legs were used to push itself through the water and may also have been used to crawl on land.

Jaekelopterus was the **biggest** sea scorpion.

MODERN **HORSESHOE CRABS** ARE MORE CLOSELY RELATED TO THE EURYPTERIDS THAN TO CRABS.

THE DISCOVERY OF SOME **EURYPTERID TRACKWAYS** SUGGEST THAT THEY MAY HAVE VENTURED ON LAND.

WHAT WAS THE LARGEST
FLIGHTLESS
BIRD?

Scientists think that the largest and heaviest of all prehistoric flightless birds was *Vorombe*. This massive bird belonged to an extinct group of flightless birds called "elephant birds", which lived on the island of Madagascar alongside a variety of strange animals, including giant lemurs, pygmy hippos, and giant tortoises. The last of the elephant birds went extinct about 1,000 years ago.

At about 1.3 m (4 ft) tall, the emperor penguin is the tallest and heaviest living penguin.

Vorombe was as tall as three emperor penguins standing on each other's shoulders and weighed a whopping 730 kg (1,600 lb). Bones of *Vorombe* were first described in 1894, but scientists thought it belonged to a different elephant bird called *Aepyornis*. It wasn't until 2018 that *Vorombe titan* was recognized as a new species.

TERROR BIRDS

Another group of large flightless birds were the phorusrhacids, also known as the "terror birds". Unlike the elephant birds, the terror birds were carnivores. They had giant skulls with large, hooked beaks that were used for slicing through meat. Some types, such as *Titanis* and *Phorusrhacos*, were top predators that chased down their prey. Some terror birds might have hit speeds of 50 kph (30 mph).

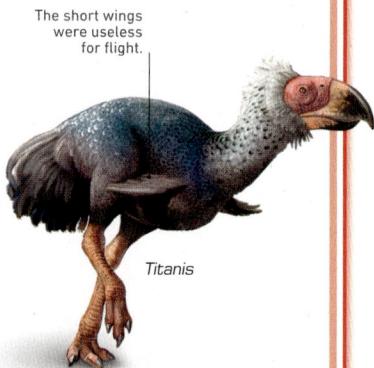

The short wings were useless for flight.

Titanis

SOME PREHISTORIC PENGUINS, SUCH AS *PALAEEUDYPTES*, WERE TALLER THAN AN ADULT HUMAN.

THE EGGS OF ELEPHANT BIRDS HAVE BEEN FOUND PRESERVED IN MUD NEAR RIVERS, LYING IN DESERTS, AND IN DENSE FORESTS.

Vorombe used its large beak to feed on fruits, roots, and shrubs.

At 3 m (10 ft) tall, *Vorombe* was the largest prehistoric flightless bird.

Tiny wings were buried under a large coat of thick feathers.

Thick, powerful legs supported *Vorombe*'s heavy body.

FAST FACTS

One of the largest flying bird to have ever existed was the vulture-like *Argentavis*. It lived about 7 MYA, soaring over the grasslands of Argentina. It had a wingspan of about 6 m (20 ft) — twice the size of the largest living bird, the wandering albatross.

Argentavis had a sharp, hooked beak for tearing into prey.

Seriemas are thought to be the only surviving relatives of terror birds. They are sometimes kept amongst chickens by South American farmers to deter predators with their loud yelping calls.

The ostrich is the largest bird in the world and, as birds evolved from dinosaurs, it is also the largest living dinosaur.

BIRDS WERE THE SECOND GROUP OF BACKBONED ANIMALS TO EVOLVE FLIGHT, AFTER THE FLYING REPTILES – THE PTEROSAURS.

MANY OF THE BIRDS THAT EVOLVED DURING THE PALEOGENE PERIOD, INCLUDING PENGUINS AND CORMORANTS, ARE STILL ALIVE TODAY.

This prehistoric giant was related to today's **ducks and geese**.

AUSTRALIAN GIANTS

As recently as the last ice age, gigantic flightless birds roamed the open woodlands of Australia. An adult male *Dromornis* could stand almost 3 m (10 ft) tall, and weigh a colossal 580 kg (1,280 lb). It had a huge bill that it probably used to gather and crush tough-skinned fruit and seeds, but it may have snacked on carrion as well, plus any small prey it could catch. The males may also have used their bills to fight each other or drive other animals out of their feeding territory.

WHAT WAS THE LARGEST
FLYING REPTILE?

Pterosaurs were the first reptiles to conquer the skies. The largest members of this spectacular group belonged to a family of Cretaceous pterosaurs called Azhdarchidae, which included the largest flying reptiles of all time. As tall as a giraffe, the pterosaur *Quetzalcoatlus* is a contender for the largest flying animal to have ever lived. A few other giant pterosaurs may have been larger, including *Arambourgiania* and *Hatzegopteryx*, but far less complete remains of these animals have been found, so palaeontologists cannot be certain.

An extra-long fourth finger bone formed the leading edge of the wing.

The crest may have been brightly coloured.

Quetzalcoatlus's body was covered in fine, hair-like filaments called pycnofibres.

The wing was made up of soft tissue.

Quetzalcoatlus was one of the **largest** flying reptiles.

Stretching 11 m (36 ft), the wings of *Quetzalcoatlus* were bigger than most small planes. Despite its monstrous size, it only weighed about 250 kg (550 lb) – about five times less than the weight of an adult giraffe. It was able to take off and soar over the land thanks to its lightweight hollow bones.

QUETZALCOATLUS WAS NAMED AFTER THE AZTEC FEATHERED SERPENT GOD **QUETZALCOATL.**

SCIENTISTS ESTIMATE THAT *QUETZALCOATLUS* WOULD HAVE BEEN ABLE TO REACH SPEEDS OF **90 KPH (56 MPH).**

LAND PREDATOR

Quetzalcoatlus may have spent a lot of time hunting on the ground, dining on a variety of animals, including small dinosaurs. It walked on its hands and feet, folding its wings against its sides and probably used its large, sharp beak like a stork to grab its prey before swallowing it whole.

The sharp, toothless beak was about 2.5 m (8 ft) long.

Small prey, including small dinosaurs, would have been easy targets.

Quetzalcoatlus

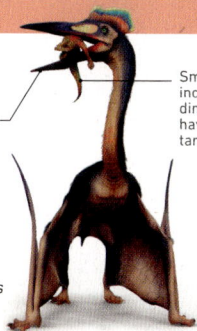

The two-seater Tiger Moth has a wingspan of 8.9 m (29 ft).

FAST FACTS

When it comes to the tallest living land animal, the giraffe holds the world record. With a height of 6 m (20 ft), it towers over the trees of the African savannah, browsing on food other animals can't reach.

QUETZALCOATLUS MAY HAVE BEEN ABLE TO FLY A STAGGERING 16,000 KM (10,000 MILES) WITHOUT STOPPING.

THE NECK VERTEBRA OF *QUETZALCOATLUS* LOOKED A BIT LIKE A TEDDY BEAR.

Pteranodon means "wings without teeth".

HIGH FLYER

The earliest pterosaurs were no bigger than crows, but by the Late Cretaceous period the skies were being patrolled by huge animals like *Pteranodon*. It had a wingspan of up to 6.5 m (21 ft), and a long, pointed, toothless beak that it used to seize fish, its main prey. Both males and females had bony crests extending from the backs of their heads, but the crests of adult males were much bigger. *Pteranodon* lived in North America, hunting near the shores of an inland sea that once divided the continent in two.

WHAT WAS THE LARGEST
AQUATIC REPTILE?

Although some of them looked like dolphins, ichthyosaurs were a group of aquatic reptiles that first flourished in the Triassic oceans. They were also the first sea animals to reach truly gigantic sizes and, with a length of 21 m (69 ft), *Shonisaurus sikanniensis* is the largest known aquatic reptile. A partial skeleton was unearthed in the late 1990s in British Columbia, Canada. The fossilized remains included a gigantic skull and a large portion of the body.

African elephants reach lengths of up to 7 m (23 ft).

The long snout was packed with large teeth that were perfect for trapping slippery prey.

The fins were like rudders, helping the ichthyosaur steer through the water.

20 ICHTHYOSAURS APPEARED ABOUT 20 MILLION YEARS BEFORE THE DINOSAURS.

LIKE DOLPHINS AND WHALES, ICHTHYOSAURS HAD TO SWIM TO THE SURFACE TO BREATHE AIR.

The length of three adult African elephants, and only slightly smaller than the biggest animal ever on the planet – the blue whale – *Shonisaurus sikanniensis* was a true giant of its day. It cruised the world's oceans, searching for prey to fuel its enormous body. A streamlined hunter, it was armed with a long snout that was perfect for snapping fish, squid, and other large marine reptiles.

The gigantic caudal fin moved from side to side, propelling *Shonisaurus* through the water.

FAST FACTS

More than 100 ichthyosaurs have been found with preserved embryos inside. Most of them come from a Jurassic fossil site in Germany, including this incredible fossil. It shows a female *Stenopterygius* giving birth to her offspring tail-first.

Offspring

Stenopterygius

Shonisaurus sikanniensis was the **largest** aquatic reptile.

NEW DISCOVERY

In 2018, a team of palaeontologists studied the remains of a large jawbone found in England. By analysing this bone and others found in the 1800s, the team concluded that they belonged to a giant ichthyosaur, which may have measured more than 30 m (98 ft) long. However, more complete fossils are needed to confirm the enormous size.

The lower jawbone was 1 m (3 ft) long.

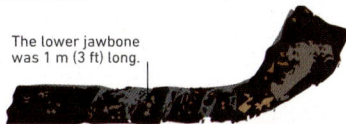

SHONISAURUS SKELETONS WERE FIRST DISCOVERED IN NEVADA, USA, IN THE **1920S**.

THE FIRST ICHTHYOSAURS WERE LESS THAN 1 M (3 FT) LONG – HALF THE SIZE OF AN ADULT HUMAN.

WHICH SEA CREATURE HAD
THE LONGEST NECK?

Plesiosaurs were sea reptiles that spent their entire lives in the watery world, even giving birth to live young at sea. With a total body length of 12 m (39 ft), about as long as a bus, *Albertonectes* was one of the longest plesiosaurs ever. It cruised the seas around what is now North America about 70 MYA, on the look out for squid and other marine animals to snap up.

The tail was a lot shorter than its neck and fossil evidence suggests that this marine reptile may have had a tail fin too.

The flippers moved up and down like wings, helping to propel *Albertonectes* through the water.

TRIASSIC PUZZLE

Since its discovery in the 1850s, palaeontologists have puzzled over the identity and lifestyle of the Triassic long-necked reptile *Tanystropheus*. It may have lived both on land and in the sea, where it would have dined on fish and squid.

The neck was about 3 m (10 ft) long.

Although a skull has never been found, *Albertonectes* would have had sharp, curved teeth similar to those of other plesiosaurs that were perfect for trapping slippery prey. Its astonishingly long neck was about 7 m (23 m) in length and made up almost two-thirds of its entire body. In total, the neck consisted of a record-breaking 76 bones. By comparison, humans have just 7 neck bones.

BITE MARKS AND SHED TEETH FROM A **SHARK** WERE FOUND ON *ALBERTONECTES*'S SKELETON.

THE GASTROLITHS SWALLOWED BY *ALBERTONECTES* WEIGHED UP TO 1 KG (2 LB).

FAST FACTS

Only one skeleton of *Albertonectes* has been found so far, and it showed that it had swallowed stones called gastroliths. These stones may have helped with digestion, grinding up food inside the gut.

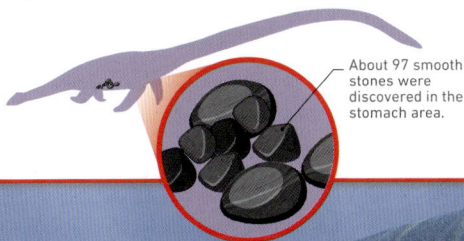

About 97 smooth stones were discovered in the stomach area.

Pliosaurs were relatives of plesiosaurs. They had short necks and massive jaws studded with huge sharp teeth. These ferocious predators hunted big sea creatures, including plesiosaurs.

The short-necked pliosaur *Liopleurodon* reached lengths of up to 8 m (26 ft).

Study of the neck bones suggests that *Albertonectes*'s neck would not have been any more flexible than a sauropod's neck.

Sharply pointed teeth

Albertonectes had the **longest neck** of any known sea creature.

A 78-MILLION-YEAR-OLD **PLESIOSAUR FOSSIL** DISCOVERED IN KANSAS, USA, HAD AN EMBRYO PRESERVED INSIDE.

FIVE FINGER-LIKE BONES SUPPORTED THE **FLIPPERS**. THESE WERE SIMILAR TO THOSE OF LIVING WHALES.

Plesiosaurus was the **first** long-necked sea reptile to be discovered.

HIDDEN TREASURE

English fossil collector Mary Anning (1799–1847) spent her life searching for fossils and discovered some of the largest prehistoric sea creatures known. Anning began hunting fossils at the age of five. She helped her father search for fossils to sell for extra money for the family. He taught her how to spot fossils on the beach and then clean them. This incredible 200-million-year-old skeleton of *Plesiosaurus* was discovered by Anning in 1823. *Plesiosaurus* lived in the shallow seas of what is now Europe during the Jurassic Period.

Pliosaurus had the **strongest** bite of any marine reptile.

The jaws opened wide enough to devour animals as large as a submersible.

Studded with rows of sharp-pointed teeth, the strong jaws closed on prey like a trap.

WHICH MARINE REPTILE HAD THE
STRONGEST BITE?

The biggest marine reptiles were formidable hunters, with massively powerful jaws and teeth that made them the oceanic equivalents of killer dinosaurs like *Tyrannosaurus*. One of the most deadly was *Pliosaurus*, a Jurassic giant with immensely long jaws that preyed on big fish and other marine reptiles. Its teeth were sharp spikes, like the teeth of a crocodile, adapted for seizing slippery prey and gripping it tightly as it struggled in vain to escape.

PLIOSAURUS **WEIGHED** AS MUCH AS 20 TONNES (22 TONS) – TWICE AS MUCH AS A BIG AFRICAN ELEPHANT.

10 THE FOSSILS OF A HUGE *PLIOSAURUS* DISCOVERED IN ENGLAND IN 1994 TOOK **10 YEARS** TO PIECE TOGETHER.

Growing to lengths of 10 m (33 ft) or more, *Pliosaurus* was one of the biggest marine predators of all time. Its fearsome jaws could grip prey with almost four times the force of a modern crocodile's bite. It might have been able to rip larger victims apart, but since its teeth were not adapted for cutting it probably swallowed most of its prey whole.

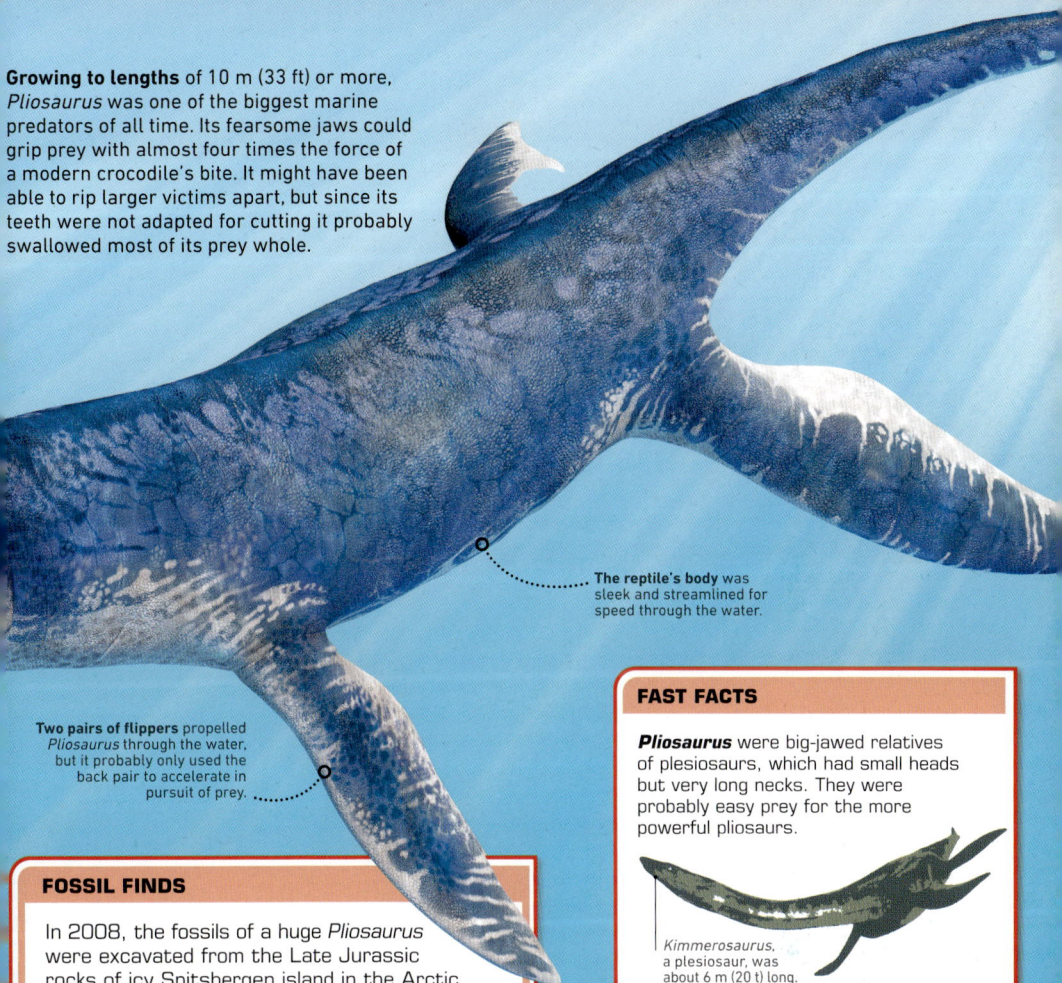

The reptile's body was sleek and streamlined for speed through the water.

Two pairs of flippers propelled *Pliosaurus* through the water, but it probably only used the back pair to accelerate in pursuit of prey.

FAST FACTS

Pliosaurus were big-jawed relatives of plesiosaurs, which had small heads but very long necks. They were probably easy prey for the more powerful pliosaurs.

Kimmerosaurus, a plesiosaur, was about 6 m (20 t) long.

Pliosaurs became extinct about 90 MYA, and the mosasaurs took over as top marine predators. These fast-swimming hunters survived until the end of the dinosaur era.

The 15-m (49-ft) long *Mosasaurus* was a ferocious predator.

FOSSIL FINDS

In 2008, the fossils of a huge *Pliosaurus* were excavated from the Late Jurassic rocks of icy Spitsbergen island in the Arctic Ocean. Repeated freezing and thawing of the rocks over 145 million years had shattered the fossils into some 20,000 fragments.

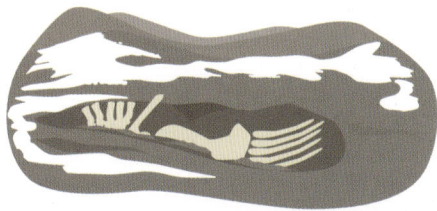

THE **FIRST** *PLIOSAURUS* FOSSILS TO BE FOUND WERE DESCRIBED BY SCIENTIST RICHARD OWEN IN 1841.

30

THE POINTED **TEETH** OF *PLIOSAURUS* WERE UP TO 30 CM (12 IN) LONG, INCLUDING THEIR ROOTS.

WHAT WAS THE LARGEST
PREHISTORIC SNAKE?

The first *Titanoboa* fossils were found in 2004 and all of the remains, including the bones from the spine, ribs, and skull, were found inside a coal mine in northern Colombia. It was a true giant of its time, reaching 14 m (46 ft) in length – longer than a school bus. Feasting on giant turtles and crocodiles would have been easy work for this massive snake – it was equipped with flexible jaws that enabled it to swallow its prey whole.

Titanoboa **was the largest snake that ever lived.**

The thickest part of *Titanoboa*'s body was at least 1 m (3 ft) wide – it would struggle to fit through your front door.

HOW DID IT EAT?

All the big snakes in the world today are found in hot climates near the equator. Scientists think that *Titanoboa*'s mega size shows that the climate would have been far warmer than it is today. *Titanoboa* lived in the tropical swamps and rainforests of South America, a habitat similar to the Amazon rainforest.

Equator

Amazon Rainforest

As its names suggests, *Titanoboa* was the largest, heaviest snake that ever lived on the planet – it was almost twice the length of one of the largest snakes alive today, the green anaconda, and weighed more than 1 tonne (1 ton), the weight of a small family car.

THE OLDEST FOSSIL SNAKES ARE AROUND 170 MILLION YEARS OLD AND COME FROM THE JURASSIC PERIOD.

20

SEVERAL EXPEDITIONS TO THE FOSSIL SITE IN COLOMBIA UNEARTHED MORE THAN 20 *TITANOBOAS*.

The massive head was 40 cm (16 in) long.

The jaws of *Titanoboa* were filled with sharp, backward-facing teeth, which were used to trap prey.

FAST FACTS

Most species of snake lay eggs, but others give birth to live young. The female yellow-bellied sea snake, for example, gives birth to about 10 live young in the open ocean, where they spend their entire lives.

The paddle-like tail enables the snake to move through the water.

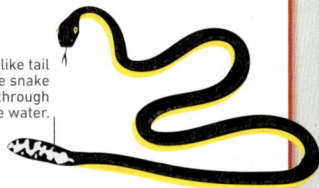

Yellow-bellied sea snake

There are about 3,800 species of snake and only 600 are venomous. Snakes use their venom for hunting and defence. Some snakes, including the Australian inland taipan, have a bite powerful enough to kill a human.

A venomous bite from the inland taipan is enough to kill 100 people.

Inland taipan

The body is about 30 cm (12 in) in diameter.

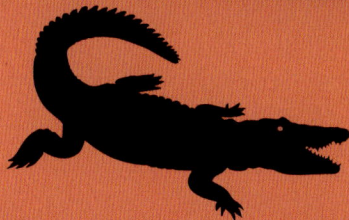

The green anaconda is about 9 m (29 ft) long.

SCIENTISTS AT FIRST THOUGHT THE COLOSSAL *TITANOBOA* FOSSILS WERE THE REMAINS OF A CROCODILE.

DEADLY COILS

Just like all the big snakes living today, *Titanoboa* could kill a crocodile or similar prey by coiling around it and squeezing tighter every time its victim breathed out. Before long, the animal would not be able to breathe at all and die of suffocation. Then *Titanoboa* would open its mouth wide to engulf its prize, using its sharp teeth to slowly drag the animal down its throat and swallow it whole. Such a big meal would take a long time to digest, and it might be weeks before *Titanoboa* needed to hunt again.

Titanoboa probably lurked in or near water, seizing prey like crocodiles and big fish.

HOW BIG WERE A
MEGALODON'S JAWS?

At 20 m (66 ft) in length – four times longer than a great white shark – *Otodus* was the largest shark to have ever lived. Also known by its species name, megalodon, it roamed the seas about 20 million years ago, shredding its prey with its gigantic jaws. Today, megalodon teeth have been found in their hundreds across the world. These extraordinary fossils help paint a picture of what these apex predators actually looked like.

Compared to the jaws of a great white shark – the deadliest shark in the world today – megalodon's jaws were massive. They were at least 3 m (10 ft) in diameter and lined with 276 teeth that were perfect for slicing through the flesh of any prey that happened to cross its path. With a bite force five times more powerful than *Tyrannosaurus*, it had the strongest biting power of any animal, living or extinct.

The massive jaws were lined with rows of razor-sharp teeth, which were replaced every 7–14 days.

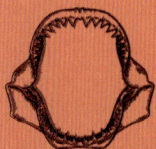

FAST FACTS

Teeth fossils from about 28 baby megalodons were found in modern-day Panama. The 400 teeth belonged to baby sharks that were between 2 and 10.5 m (6 and 34 ft) in length and are thought to be from a shark nursery, where megalodon families lived for protection.

The largest of the baby shark fossils was about five times the size of an adult human.

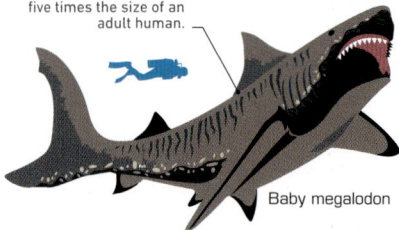

Baby megalodon

NO COMPLETE MEGALODON FOSSIL HAS BEEN FOUND, SO SCIENTISTS ESTIMATE THE SHARK'S JAW SIZE BASED ON THE SIZE OF ITS TEETH.

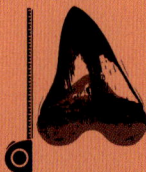

THE BIGGEST MEGALODON TOOTH EVER FOUND IS 19 CM (7.48 IN) IN LENGTH.

A MEGA MYSTERY

Megalodon died out about 3.5 MYA, but scientists are still unsure why. The mega shark may have been killed off by a period of global cooling — it liked warmer waters and as the planet cooled there may not have been enough food for megalodon. Other predators like the great white shark, which lived at the same time, would have competed with megalodon for food, and this may also have helped to drive it to extinction.

Great white shark

The largest of the triangular, serrated teeth were about the size of an adult human hand.

The teeth were similar to those of a great white shark.

Megalodon's jaws were big enough for a **family car** to drive through.

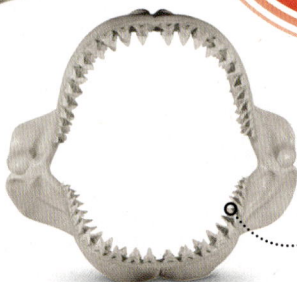

A great white shark's tooth is 5 cm (2 in) long.

Megalodon's jaw

Great white shark's jaw

A **SHARK'S JAWS** ARE CONNECTED LOOSELY TO ITS SKULL. THIS ENABLES IT TO PUSH OUT ITS JAWS AND TAKE A HUGE CHUNK OUT OF ITS PREY.

BASED ON ITS SIZE, MEGALODON WOULD HAVE EATEN ABOUT **1,130 KG** (2,500 LB) OF FOOD EVERY DAY.

SHOCK AND AWE

Just like its living relative, the modern great white shark, megalodon was the most powerful marine predator of its time. But it was far bigger than a great white, so would have had no trouble killing and eating any animal it encountered, including these giant sperm whales. Like a great white, megalodon was a fast swimmer, easily able to overpower its terrified prey. They had no defence as it charged into the attack, slicing into a victim and inflicting such terrible injuries that the animal died of shock almost instantly.

Megalodon **hunted** in warm and temperate oceans all over the world.

ICE-AGE MARSUPIALS

Like many of the early mammals, *Thylacinus* was a marsupial — a pouched mammal like modern-day koalas and kangaroos. While most of the ice-age marsupials became extinct about 30,000 years ago, *Thylacinus* survived until the early 1900s.

Thylacinus had distinctive stripes along its back and tail.

Thylacinus

WHAT WAS LIFE LIKE
IN THE ICE AGE?

The last Ice Age, which lasted from 110,000 to 12,000 years ago, was a time when many big, spectacular mammals roamed the world. The shaggy-haired woolly mammoth lived on cold grasslands all around the Arctic, alongside wild horses and bison. Further south, sabre-toothed cats preyed on other giant plant-eaters, while mega-sized marsupials were thriving in South America and Australia.

Glyptodon

As big as a small car, *Glyptodon* was a heavily armoured relative of modern armadillos and lived on the grassy plains of South America until about 12,000 years ago. It relied on its tough bony shell as its main form of defence against predators like the sabre-toothed cats.

Diprotodon

Standing almost 2.1 m (7 ft) tall, the giant wombat *Diprotodon* was the size of a rhinoceros. It had enormous front teeth, which it would have used to rip the leaves from bushes and trees in the woodlands of its native Australia.

Diprotodon was the biggest marsupial that ever lived.

These solid, bony plates were about 2.5 cm (1 inch) thick.

THE LAST WILD ***THYLACINUS*** WAS KILLED BY A FARMER IN TASMANIA IN 1930.

THE BONY SHELLS OF *GLYPTODON* WERE BIG ENOUGH FOR ICE-AGE PEOPLE TO USE AS SHELTERS.

The mammoth's tusks grew to 4 m (13 ft) long and curved inward at their tips.

Woolly mammoth
Close relatives of the modern Asian elephant, mammoths had giant curved tusks and big flat teeth adapted for chewing tough grass. The most famous of them, the woolly mammoth, lived in the far north 200,000–4,000 years ago, where its shaggy coat enabled it to cope with the cold winters.

The thick hair of a woolly mammoth was up to 1 m (3 ft) long.

Smilodon may have been spotted like a leopard.

Smilodon
The sabre-toothed cat *Smilodon* lived throughout much of North and South America. It was armed with incredibly long canine teeth that it used to stab and kill big animals including camels, bison, and giant ground sloths.

WOOLLY MAMMOTHS SURVIVED ON WRANGEL ISLAND IN ARCTIC RUSSIA UNTIL ABOUT 4,000 YEARS AGO.

THOUSANDS OF *SMILODON* FOSSILS HAVE BEEN FOUND AT ONE SITE IN CALIFORNIA, USA.

Awesome animals

RECORD BREAKERS

▼ Mega predator

Reaching lengths of up to 70 cm (28 in), **Anomalocaris** lived about 500 MYA and was the largest predator of its time. It used its flattened sides like flaps to swim through the ocean, grasping passing prey with its long, curved mouthparts.

The mouthparts were lined with deadly spikes.

With its massive mouth and powerful jaws, small animals and even young dinosaurs would have been easy prey.

▲ Supersized frog

Also known as the "devil's frog", **Beelzebufo** may have been one of the largest frogs that ever lived. Lurking on the island of Madagascar during the Late Cretaceous, it was about the size of a beach ball with a deadly bite force comparable to modern-day wolves.

▼ Bone crusher

The largest meat-eating land mammal that has ever lived was a wolf-like animal called **Andrewsarchus**. It was about 4 m (13 ft) long and roamed the plains of Mongolia about 40 MYA, ripping into prey with its bone crunching teeth.

The jaws were armed with both flesh piercing teeth at the front and bone crunching teeth at the back.

COLOSSAL COUSINS

These **prehistoric creatures** are relatives of **modern-day animals** you can see today, **but much bigger.**

Procoptodon

A short-faced kangaroo that died out around **30,000 years ago** was about three times bigger than the largest kangaroos today. Instead of hopping, **Procoptodon** probably walked due to its large size.

Gigantopithecus

This **gigantic ape** was about 3 m (10 ft) tall. It thrived in the forests of what is now southern China until **100,000 years ago**. Its closest living relative is the orangutan — the largest tree-dwelling mammal.

SABRE-TOOTHED CATS HAD LONG CANINE TEETH THAT REACHED LENGTHS OF UP TO 18 CM (7 IN).

FOSSIL EVIDENCE SUGGESTS THAT HORSES MAY HAVE BEEN TAMED ABOUT 4,000 YEARS AGO BY THE PEOPLE OF CENTRAL ASIA.

DID YOU KNOW?

One of the earliest known **mammals** was a shrew-like creature that lived around 225 MYA. *Brasilodon* measured just 12 cm (5 in) in length and probably hunted insects.

Brasilodon

Horses first appeared about 54 MYA. No bigger than a fox, they lived in forests, browsing on plants and leaves. They had separate toes on each foot instead of a single hoof.

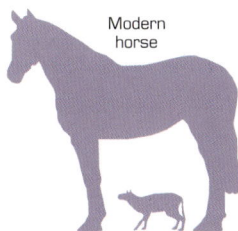

Modern horse

Early horse

The first **camels** lived in North America and had no humps, only gaining their important fat reserves about 5 MYA. Some, including *Protylopus*, were no bigger than a cat, while others were as big as horses.

Protylopus

Modern dromedary

ANIMAL ATHLETES

Super swimmer

Mosasaurs were marine reptiles that lived during the Cretaceous Period. With their powerful flippers and streamlined body, they were perfectly adapted for swimming. Scientists estimate that mosasaurs had a top speed of about **48 kph (30 mph)**.

0   48 kph (30 mph)

Rapid runner

The size of a lion, the sabre-toothed cat **Smilodon** lived during the last ice age, preying on any unsuspecting animal, including deer, camels, and horses. Although it probably stalked its prey, it may have been able to run in short bursts of up to **48 kph (30 mph)**.

0   48 kph (30 mph)

Fast flier

One of the largest ever flying birds, the **Pelagornis**, had a wingspan about the size of a school bus. Using a computer model, scientists were able to work out that the giant bird would have soared at a speedy **64 kph (40 mph)**.

0   64 kph (40 mph)

Archelon

This **sea turtle** was the size of a car. Its outer shell was leathery, like those of living leatherback sea turtles. It lived about **75 MYA**, using its huge flippers to glide through the water.

Machimosaurus

The huge jaws of this **marine crocodile** were powerful enough to crush turtle shells. It reached lengths of up to 7 m (23 ft) — the biggest marine crocodile ever. It thrived about **120 MYA**.

Arctotherium

Standing around 3 m (10 ft) tall, **Arctotherium** was the largest bear to have ever existed. It lived about **2 MYA** in South America. Its powerful jaws could crunch through bone and it may have even taken on the sabre-toothed cat.

BEELZEBUFO'S BITE FORCE WAS STRONG ENOUGH TO BREAK A HUMAN FINGER BONE.

ONLY ONE FOSSIL OF **ANDREWSARCHUS** HAS BEEN DISCOVERED — A GIANT SKULL MEASURING 83 CM (33 IN).

Fantastic fossils

Most of the animals and plants that have ever lived are extinct, and no-one has ever seen them alive. But the fossils of many survive, sometimes preserving amazing detail, and giving us a window into a vanished world.

This slab of limestone is packed with the fossils of ammonites – shelled relatives of octopuses and squid that hunted in prehistoric seas. They were wiped out by the extinction event 66 MYA, which also destroyed the giant dinosaurs.

HOW ARE FOSSILS
FORMED?

Most of what we know about dinosaurs has been worked out from fossils – the remains of their bodies that have been buried in the ground for millions of years. Over this vast length of time minerals replace the once-living tissue, turning it to stone. But this can only happen if it does not decay first, so most fossils are of teeth and bones, which are tough enough to resist decay. Only rarely do soft tissues such as skin and feathers become fossilized, giving us a glimpse of what the animals looked like when alive.

The process that creates a fossil usually occurs underwater, so fossils of land animals are much rarer than those of sea creatures. To survive as a fossil, a land animal like a dinosaur must die in a place where it is soon buried, and where water can seep into its remains and turn them to stone.

By this time all the soft body parts have decayed, leaving only teeth and bones.

The dead dinosaur sinks into the soft mud, where it is safe from scavengers.

Dinosaur dies
Most dead animals are soon eaten by hungry scavengers, which scatter their bones. But this dinosaur has fallen into a river, where its body is soon buried and hidden by mud. The lack of oxygen in the mud slows the rate of decay, making fossilization more likely.

Sediment builds up
Sand and mud carried by the water builds up on the riverbed, covering the dinosaur's body with more layers of sediment. Their weight compresses the mud containing the skeleton, eventually turning it to hard sedimentary rock.

THE WORD FOSSIL COMES FROM THE LATIN WORD *FOSSILIS*, WHICH MEANS "DUG UP."

IN 1824, THE FOSSILS OF A DINOSAUR WERE GIVEN THE NAME *MEGALOSAURUS*. THIS WAS THE FIRST DINOSAUR TO GET A SCIENTIFIC NAME.

FAST FACTS

Visitors to the Dinosaur National Monument in Utah, USA, can see more than 1,500 fossil dinosaur bones still embedded in 150-million-year-old sandstone.

Dinosaur skull fossil

Although 98 per cent of Antarctica is now covered by a massive ice sheet, five types of dinosaur have been found there, including the big hunter *Cryolophosaurus*.

Cryolophosaurus

The best fossils occur in very fine-grained rocks that preserve every tiny detail. The first fossil feathers to be discovered were found in rock of this type — the Jurassic limestone of Solnhofen in southern Germany.

Fossil preserved in limestone

The river has long since dried up, and the land above the fossil is in the grip of an ice age.

The land is now a desert, very unlike the habitat of the dead dinosaur.

The scientists draw and photograph the exposed fossil before they remove any part of it.

Fossilization
As the mud around the skeleton turns to rock, minerals dissolved in the groundwater seep into the bones. These minerals gradually replace the dead tissue, but preserve its shape. In some fossils even microscopic features are preserved in this way.

Discovery
Millions of years after the dinosaur died, erosion of the rock exposes its fossil remains. Luckily, a fossil hunter discovers them before they are destroyed by more erosion. The scientists get to work, carefully excavating the bones and recording their position before removing them for further study.

THE BONES OF BIG ANIMALS ARE MORE LIKELY TO SURVIVE AS FOSSILS THAN THE BONES OF SMALL ONES.

SOME EXTINCT ANIMALS ARE KNOWN ONLY FROM THEIR FOSSILIZED TEETH.

WHAT ARE THE DIFFERENT
TYPES OF FOSSIL?

Typical fossils are of bones, teeth, or shells that have been turned to stone, but there are other types of fossil. Some consist of an impression of something rather than its whole form. Others, such as food remains, provide evidence of how the animals lived. A few, like flies in amber, preserve the entire creature, just as it was in life.

The deposited minerals harden into stone.

Although the body is complete, substances like DNA are unlikely to survive.

Left in mud that has turned to stone, this is the footprint of a three-toed theropod dinosaur.

Natural cast
Minerals dissolved in water can build up inside a hollow object like a shell, forming a cast of its internal shape. This fossil ammonite – an extinct shelled relative of squid – formed like this.

Preserved in amber
Trapped in sticky tree resin millions of years ago, this fly has been preserved because, over time, the resin hardened into a stony form called amber. Every feature of the insect is intact – even its delicate wings.

Trace fossil
Sometimes the only evidence that an animal existed are the traces that it left behind, such as footprints. But these can be very useful since they help scientists work out how the animals moved and even how they lived together.

ANY ONCE-LIVING THING THAT SURVIVES FOR MORE THAN 10,000 YEARS IS CONSIDERED A FOSSIL.

THE ANCIENT GREEK SCHOLAR ARISTOTLE REALIZED THAT FOSSILS WERE THE REMAINS OF LIVING THINGS.

FAST FACTS

Plants are fossilized as well as animals. Entire tree trunks can turn to stone in a process known as petrification. In some places whole petrified forests are preserved, with the trees still lying where they fell.

The growth rings are still visible.

The bodies of ice-age animals like this baby mammoth have been found buried in Arctic ice. Frozen solid within a few days, they preserve soft tissues that would never normally survive, including hair and even the animal's last meal.

Mammoths were covered in long hair, which helped to keep the body warm.

This coprolite from North America is over 70 million years old.

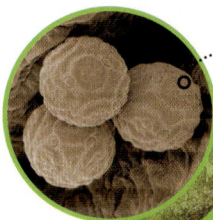

The mould of this trilobite clearly shows its segmented form.

Every detail of the pollen grain is preserved except its colour.

Coprolite
Amazingly, even animal dung can be fossilized. Known as coprolites, these trace fossils often preserve fragments of undigested food, so scientists can pull them apart to find out what an extinct dinosaur was eating.

Mould
If an animal sinks into soft mud that then turns to rock, its body may not survive. But it sometimes leaves an impression of its shape, called a mould. Such fossils often preserve the fine detail of the animal's appearance.

Pickled in peat
Waterlogged plant remains are preserved as peat for thousands of years. These peat deposits contain tiny pollen grains that can be identified under a microscope, showing scientists what was growing at the time.

TINY FOSSILS THAT CAN ONLY BE SEEN BY USING A MICROSCOPE ARE KNOWN AS MICROFOSSILS.

THE ANCIENT CHINESE THOUGHT THAT FOSSILS WERE THE BONES OF DRAGONS.

This site includes the **longest** dinosaur trackway, at 347 m (1,140 ft) long.

DINOSAUR TRAIL

This sheet of rock in South America is covered with thousands of footprints made by dinosaurs as they walked over a mudflat on the shores of a shallow lake 68 MYA. Over time, the mud turned to rock, and the massive earth movements that created the Andes mountains buckled the rock so it forms a near-vertical wall 100 m (330 ft) high. Part of a limestone quarry in Cal Orcko, Bolivia, the rock wall preserves the tracks of at least six types of dinosaur, all heading in different directions.

HOW LONG DOES AN
EXCAVATION TAKE?

Excavating a dinosaur fossil takes skill, care, and a lot of patience. Before any bones are removed their exact positions must be recorded, since they may provide valuable clues to the animal's anatomy or how it died. Only then can excavators carefully remove the fossils, reinforcing them as necessary, and pack them up for transport to a laboratory. Here they are unpacked, cleaned up, and identified. Fragile bones must often be conserved to stop them falling apart. Some may then be used to make a replica skeleton for display in a museum.

DINOSAUR SCIENCE

Every new fossil that is found may contain evidence that disproves a well-established scientific theory. For example, when the first fossils of the herbivore *Iguanodon* were found, it was assumed that a spiky bone found with them was attached to the dinosaur's nose like a rhinoceros horn. However, later evidence showed that the spike was actually part of the animal's thumb.

Iguanodon's stout thumb spike was probably for defence.

The **excavation** of a big fossil is a **slow** process – it can take many months and even years.

Many dinosaur fossils are found by accident, having been exposed by natural erosion of the rock or human activity such as quarrying. But once a site is known to contain fossils, it attracts experts who survey the site for traces of other fossils preserved by the same conditions. Some of the most famous sites have yielded hundreds of fossils found in this way. They include the Flaming Cliffs region of the Gobi Desert in Mongolia.

BECAUSE FOSSIL BONES ARE VALUABLE AND OFTEN FRAGILE, MOST OF THE SKELETONS DISPLAYED IN MUSEUMS ARE REPLICAS.

FEW FOSSIL SKELETONS ARE DISCOVERED INTACT. MOST ARE JUST A JUMBLE OF BONES THAT NEED EXPERT REASSEMBLY.

In the Gobi Desert, erosion of 75-million-year-old rocks has revealed fossils of the bird-like dinosaur *Oviraptor* and its eggs.

The *Oviraptor* eggs were long and narrow.

FAST FACTS

Although most fossils are formed of stone, they can be fragile. Before transporting them to the laboratory the excavators protect them with a covering of paper and wet plaster, called a field jacket.

The field jacket is similar to the plaster casts used by doctors to mend broken bones.

The Zhucheng fossil site in China is the most productive dinosaur fossil site found so far. More than 7,600 dinosaur bones have been discovered there, including *Sinoceratops*, an Asian relative of the mighty *Triceratops*.

Sinoceratops

The dinosaurs have been locked in combat for more than 70 million years.

In 1971, the Gobi Desert yielded one of the most exciting dinosaur fossils ever found — the skeleton of a *Velociraptor* with its clawed foot lodged in the throat of a *Protoceratops*. The pair must have been buried while still fighting.

FOSSILS COME IN ALL SIZES – FROM GIGANTIC DINOSAURS TO MICROSCOPIC BACTERIA.

SOME FOSSILS CANNOT BE IDENTIFIED EASILY, AND MAY LIE IN MUSEUMS FOR YEARS BEFORE SOMEONE REALIZES WHAT THEY ARE.

Ice-age people used mammoth **bones and tusks** to build huts.

MAMMOTH BONES

Some of the best fossil sites are places that once attracted large numbers of animals. Here, the fossil remains of a mammoth discovered in South Dakota, USA, are being excavated from a bed of rock that was once a pond in a steep-sided sinkhole. During the last ice age the water attracted thirsty animals such as bears, wolves, and mammoths. Finding themselves unable to escape, they died and were buried in mud that later turned to rock.

STUDYING POO

Some scientists spend all their time studying fossilized poo. This provides them with important clues about what prehistoric animals ate and about their behaviour. Coprolites also provide evidence of what plants and trees flourished in the past.

Coprolite collection

HOW BIG WERE
DINOSAUR POOS?

Dinosaur poo came in all shapes and sizes, and fossilized poo – known as coprolite – has been found on every continent. The world's largest is a whopper, measuring 67.5 cm (26.5 in) long. Discovered in South Dakota, USA, the coprolite was made by a large carnivore, almost certainly a *Tyrannosaurus rex*, whose bones have been found in the same layers of rock. This coprolite is nicknamed Barnum, after palaeontologist Barnum Brown who first discovered the remains of *Tyrannosaurus rex*.

PALAEONTOLOGISTS HAVE DISCOVERED SEVERAL FOSSIL SITES THAT APPEAR TO BE LATRINES, WHERE ANIMALS POOED IN ONE PLACE.

WILLIAM BUCKLAND, WHO NAMED FOSSILIZED POO COPROLITE, HAD A TABLE MADE OF COPROLITES.

FAST FACTS

In 1829, scientist William Buckland coined the word coprolite. This was based on finds made by palaeontologist Mary Anning. She had came across strange looking lumps near the fossil of an ichthyosaur on the south coast of England. When she examined the lumps, she saw they contained fish bones. Anning had discovered fossilized poo!

Mary Anning

In 2021, scientists discovered a new species of beetle in a lump of fossilized poo that is about 230 million years old. The poo is thought to come from *Silesaurus opolensis*, an early ancestor of dinosaurs. It was a small, agile hunter, perhaps feasting on both plants and animals.

Silesaurus was about 2 m (6 ft) long.

Coprolites like this may come in a variety of different colours, depending on how they formed as fossils and where they were found. Sometimes it is possible to work out who left the coprolite – the high bone content and its size suggests that a *Tyrannosaurus rex* was responsible for this record breaking coprolite left behind 66 MYA.

The **biggest** dinosaur fossilized poo is the length of seven toilet rolls.

RARE EVIDENCE OF FOSSILIZED DINOSAUR PEE TRACES HAVE BEEN FOUND IN BRAZIL AND THE USA.

DUNG BEETLES WERE AROUND DURING THE AGE OF DINOSAURS, HELPING TO CLEAR DUNG JUST AS THEY DO TODAY.

FAST FACTS

In 2015, scientists studying a fossil pterosaur found what seems to be a coprolite still inside its body. It contains what are probably the remains of squid caught at sea.

Some coprolites are so big that entire bones are preserved inside them. Some of these bones even have tooth marks made by the hunter as it devoured its prey.

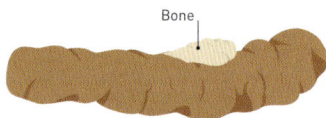

Bone

Scientists analyse coprolites by cutting them into thin slices that can be examined under a microscope. This enables them to identify all kinds of tiny items including plant pollen and fungal spores, as well as larger features like seeds, insect remains, shells, and bone fragments.

The remains of tapeworms and their eggs have been discovered in coprolites. These show that some dinosaurs were plagued by parasitic worms that lived in their guts and feasted on the food they ate.

Some plant material is difficult to digest and passes right through an animal almost unaltered. This helps us see exactly what types of plant a dinosaur was eating.

POO DECAYS QUICKLY, SO IT HAS TO BE BURIED SOMEWHERE AIRLESS TO HAVE ANY CHANCE OF BEING FOSSILIZED.

FISH SCALES AND HOOKS FROM SQUID SUCKERS HAVE BEEN FOUND IN THE **COPROLITES** OF ANCIENT MARINE REPTILES.

WHAT'S BEEN FOUND INSIDE
DINOSAUR POO?

We can work out what dinosaurs ate by looking at their teeth, but the food fragments found in coprolites – fossilized poo – can tell us a lot more. Some of these were clearly left by dinosaurs that fed on plants or insects, while others are laced with the remains of big animals. Some even contain parasites that lived inside dinosaurs. But since we have never found a fossilized dinosaur actually pooing, it's difficult to know what poo belonged to which dinosaur!

The hard body parts of insects such as beetles have been preserved virtually intact in some coprolites, giving scientists valuable information about ancient insect life.

Bone fragments found in a big coprolite are evidence that the poo probably belonged to a powerful hunter like *Tyrannosaurus*.

FOSSILIZED FARTS

Fossilized tree resin, known as amber, can contain whole insects that were trapped in the sticky resin oozing from trees millions of years ago. Some of these unfortunate insects have been preserved passing wind! After they got stuck, the gas inside their tiny bodies was released and formed bubbles in the resin, which then hardened around them.

Fossilized fart bubbles

PHOSPHATE IS A MAJOR INGREDIENT OF BONE, SO COPROLITES CONTAINING IT ARE THE FOSSILIZED POO OF MEAT-EATERS.

IN THE PAST, COPROLITES WERE GROUND UP FOR USE AS **FERTILIZER**.

FAST FACTS

Footprint fossils that are about 113 million years old were discovered in a dry riverbed in Texas, USA, in 2022. They show that a colossal *Sauroposeidon* was being stalked by *Acrocanthosaurus*, a relative of *Tyrannosaurus*.

Three-toed footprint of *Acrocanthosaurus*

The **largest** dinosaur footprint could fit an adult human inside it.

FOSSILIZED DINOSAUR TRACKS HAVE BEEN FOUND ON EVERY CONTINENT, INCLUDING **ANTARCTICA**.

THE **STRIDE LENGTH** OF THE PLANT-EATING *BRACHIOSAURUS* WAS ABOUT 1.8 M (6 FT).

WHAT'S THE LARGEST
DINOSAUR
FOOTPRINT?

As well as fossilized bones, some dinosaurs left clues of their existence in the form of footprints, or trace fossils. These amazing tracks provide a snapshot of how they lived. Lots of overlapping footprints found together, for example, show that some dinosaurs travelled in herds. Sets of tracks have also shown that they protected their young by keeping them in the middle of the group. Tracks that are further apart show how fast dinosaurs ran, while tracks closer together show how they walked.

Thousands of dinosaur tracks belonging to 21 different individuals were discovered at a site in western Australia in 2017. One of those tracks measured a whopping 1.7 m (5 ft 6 in) long and is thought to be the largest ever found. The print was from the hind foot of a giant sauropod that was about 5 m (16 ft) tall.

FOOTPRINT CLUES

Each dinosaur group had distinctive tracks, so palaeontologists are able to identify the trackmaker by looking at the shape, the number of toes, and the spacing of the footprints.

Sauropods were the heavyweights of the dinosaur world. They left behind large, round, and deep footprints. Their handprints were smaller.

Theropods were agile hunters. They had slender three-toed claws that made a distinctive V-shaped pattern.

Ornithopods' footprints show they didn't have claws. Their toes were also rounded and more spaced apart than those of theropods.

Ankylosaurs created deep-set tracks. These tracks also show that they had three or four toes and five fingers.

Ceratopsians had four toes and five fingers. Their tracks were also more rounded than those of ankylosaurs.

FOOTPRINTS FOUND IN SPAIN IN 2021 SHOW THAT THEY WERE MADE BY A THEROPOD RUNNING AT ABOUT 45 KPH (28 MPH).

IN SOME PARTS OF THE WORLD, INCLUDING GANTHEAUME POINT IN AUSTRALIA, **DINOSAUR TRACKS** CAN BE SEEN AT LOW TIDE.

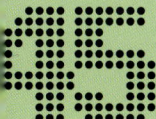

FAST FACTS

The first dinosaurs probably ate a variety of food. These early dinosaurs gave rise to more specialized predators like the meat-eating *Herrerasaurus* and plant-eaters like *Thecodontosaurus*.

Thecodontosaurus

Nyasasaurus likely had a really long tail that was half the length of its body.

WHAT'S THE OLDEST
DINOSAUR FOSSIL?

Every year, new discoveries change what we know about dinosaurs, from when they lived to what they looked like. It was once thought that dinosaurs appeared on the planet about 230 MYA, but a discovery in 2012 pushed that date back by between 10 and 15 million years. The first dinosaurs were probably small predators that walked on two feet with grasping hands. At the time, not many of these animals existed on the planet. It wasn't until 201 MYA, at the beginning of the Jurassic Period, when dinosaurs really started to thrive.

NYASASAURUS'S BONE TISSUE SHOWS THAT IT INCREASED IN SIZE RAPIDLY – A KEY FEATURE OF EARLY DINOSAURS.

THE 230-MILLION-YEAR-OLD FOSSIL OF THE SMALL DINOSAUR *MBIRESAURUS*, SHOWED THAT IT WAS AN EARLY RELATIVE OF THE GIANT SAUROPODS.

Spine bones

First discovered in modern-day Tanzania in the 1930s, *Nyasasaurus* is known from one upper arm bone and just six vertebrae (spine bones). The bones were locked away in the storerooms of the Natural History Museum in London for more than half a century before being re-examined in 2012. At around 243 million years old, *Nyasasaurus* is thought to be the oldest dinosaur fossil ever found.

ARCHOSAURS

During the Early Triassic period, about 240 MYA, the crocodile-like reptiles called archosaurs dominated life on Earth. This diverse group of animals included the powerfully built *Postosuchus*, the top predator of its time. Others, including *Marasuchus*, were small, slender, and agile animals. Dinosaurs, pterosaurs, and crocodiles evolved from archosaurs, sharing features that make it hard for scientists to tell them apart.

Postosuchus had sharp, serrated teeth that were perfect for tearing into prey.

Postosuchus

Marasuchus was only 70 cm (28 in) long.

Marasuchus

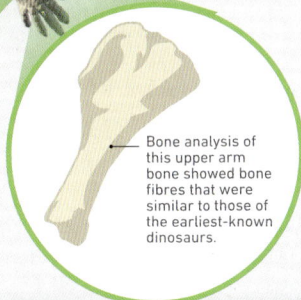

Bone analysis of this upper arm bone showed bone fibres that were similar to those of the earliest-known dinosaurs.

THE **OLDEST HUMAN FOSSILS** HAVE BEEN FOUND IN SOUTH AFRICA. THE SITE IS KNOWN AS THE CRADLE OF HUMANKIND.

400

THE FOSSIL OF *RHYNIOGNATHA*, AN INSECT THAT LIVED 400 MYA, IS THE OLDEST KNOWN FOSSIL OF AN INSECT.

HAS A COMPLETE DINOSAUR FOSSIL
BEEN FOUND?

Tyrannosaurus rex is one of the most recognizable dinosaurs on the planet, and there's no specimen more famous than Sue. Discovered in 1990 on a ranch in South Dakota, USA, almost all of the dinosaur's bones were accounted for and they proved just how massive these ferocious predators were.

The skull weighs 272 kg (600 lb) and is too heavy to be placed on top of the skeleton, so it is kept in a separate case and a replica is used instead.

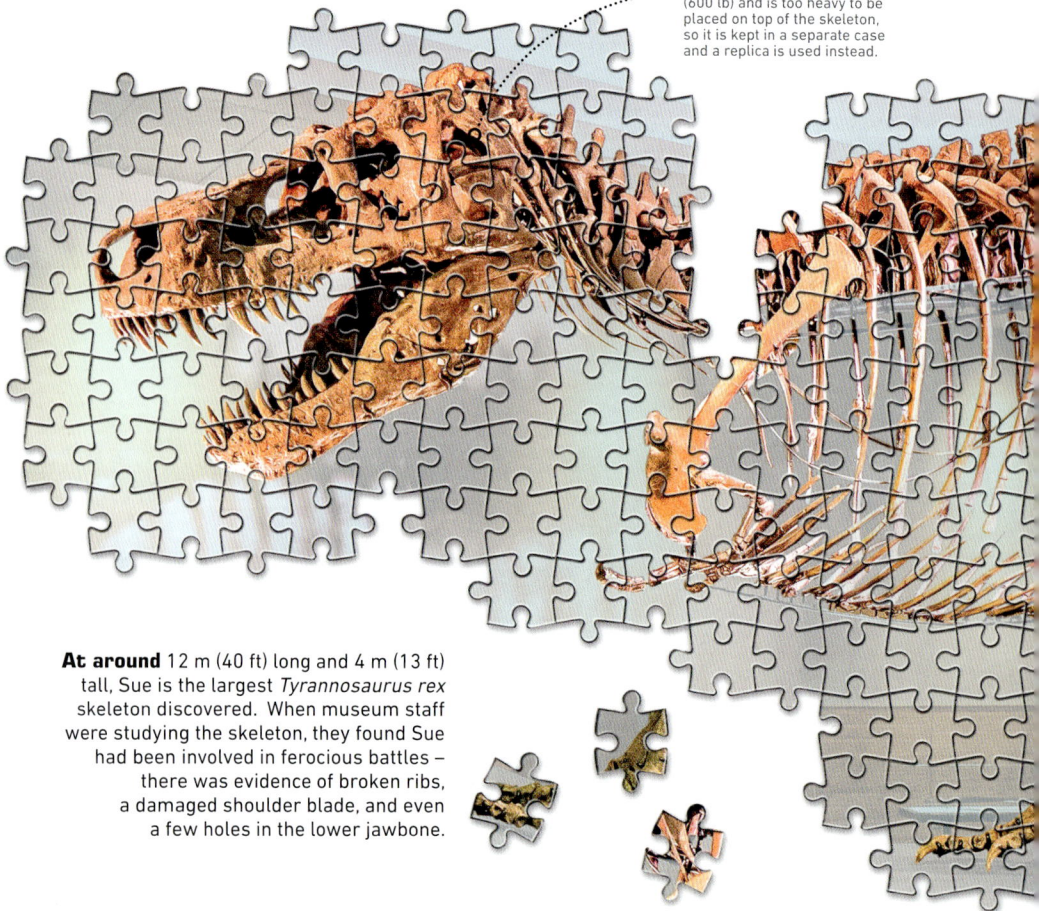

At around 12 m (40 ft) long and 4 m (13 ft) tall, Sue is the largest *Tyrannosaurus rex* skeleton discovered. When museum staff were studying the skeleton, they found Sue had been involved in ferocious battles – there was evidence of broken ribs, a damaged shoulder blade, and even a few holes in the lower jawbone.

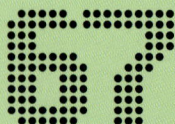

67 FOR ABOUT 67 MILLION YEARS, SUE HAD BEEN **BURIED** IN MUDROCK, WHICH KEPT THE BONES SAFE FROM SCAVENGERS.

IT TOOK TWELVE MUSEUM STAFF **50,000 HOURS** TO PREPARE SUE FOR A MUSEUM DISPLAY

FAST FACTS

Despite being called Sue, scientists are unsure whether the dinosaur was male or female. It was named after the palaeontologist — Sue Hendrickson — who stumbled across the bones of *T. rex*, jutting out from a cliff face.

A *Triceratops* that died during the Late Cretaceous was discovered in Montana, USA, in 2014. Palaeontologists excavated more than 260 bones — that's about 85 per cent of the skeleton. Named Horridus, it is one of the most complete *Triceratops* fossil in the world.

Sue's left shin bone was twice the size of the right. This was probably due to the fact that it had become infected.

With **90%** of the skeleton, Sue is the most complete dinosaur fossil ever discovered.

28
SCIENTISTS ESTIMATE THAT SUE WAS ABOUT **28 YEARS OLD** WHEN SHE DIED.

MORE THAN 50 *T. REX* SPECIMENS HAVE BEEN FOUND IN PRESENT-DAY WESTERN USA.

Fossil finds

IMPORTANT FOSSIL FINDS

Tiktaalik

Fishapod
Also called a "fishapod", **Tiktaalik** lived about 375 MYA. It had features of a fish as well as those of a tetrapod, a four-legged animal. It had lungs and gills, leg-like fins and scales, and could swim or crawl on land. Its discovery showed how **tetrapods evolved from fish**.

Pakicetus

First whale
Cetaceans — a group of marine mammals that include whales and dolphins — didn't always look like they do today. The **first cetaceans, like *Pakicetus*, looked more like bears or wolves and lived on land.** *Pakicetus* lived in modern-day Pakistan more than 50 MYA.

Caudipteryx

Dino-bird
Amazing dinosaur fossils from the Cretaceous Period have been unearthed in **Liaoning, China.** These fossils show that instead of scales many dinosaurs had feathers — evidence that **birds evolved from dinosaurs**.

SUPERSIZED DINO DIG

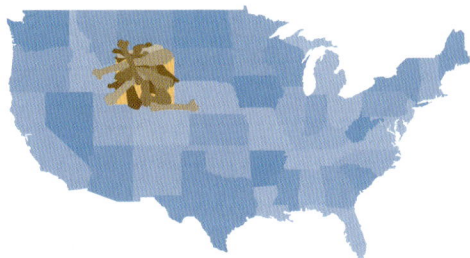

One of the most important excavations in recent years is **Mission Jurassic** — a treasure trove of dinosaur fossils in north Wyoming, USA. The dig, which started in 2019, is expected to last **20 years** and will uncover more secrets about dinosaurs that lived during the Jurassic Period.

ANCIENT FOREST

About **160 MYA**, during the Middle Jurassic period, huge **forests of *Araucaria*** towered over parts of Patagonia in Argentina.

Trees reaching 100 m (330 ft) tall dominated the woodlands in an area known as **Cerro Cuadrado**, until a volcano erupted and buried the site. Over the years, the trees in the forest petrified ("turned to stone"). Today, the Cerro Cuadrado Petrified Forest is one of the **best preserved forest ecosystems** from the Jurassic Period.

THE FIRST COMPLETE DINOSAUR SKELETON TO BE MOUNTED IN A MUSEUM WAS A *HADROSAURUS* IN 1868.

THE WORLD'S LARGEST DINOSAUR GRAVEYARD IN CANADA IS ABOUT THE SIZE OF 280 FOOTBALL PITCHES.

LIVING
FOSSILS

Some animals alive today haven't changed much in **millions of years of evolution**. These animals give us a glimpse of what **prehistoric creatures looked like**.

Horseshoe crab

Despite their name, these creatures **aren't crabs at all**. They are more **closely related to spiders and other arachnids**. They have lived on Earth almost unchanged for **445 million years**.

Coelacanth

The **coelacanths** belonged to an ancient group of fish that first appeared about 360 MYA. Scientists thought they went **extinct 66 MYA**, along with the dinosaurs, but in 1938, a fisherman caught a **living coelacanth**.

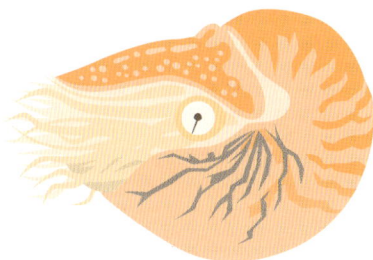

Fig wasps

These **wasps** can travel further than any other insect — flying about **160 km (100 miles)** in two days. They are such efficient fliers, they haven't changed much over **60 million years**.

Nautilus

Marine molluscs like this have been around longer than four-legged animals, insects, and trees. They have roamed the oceans almost unchanged for **500 million years**, using their tentacles to grasp passing prey.

DUELLING
DINOSAURS

The Duelling Dinosaurs were discovered tangled in a lump of sandstone.

One of the most amazing fossils discovered in the past 20 years shows a young *Tyrannosaurus* and a *Triceratops* probably locked in battle.

Known as the **Duelling Dinosaurs**, the fossil was discovered in Montana, USA, in 2006. It is the most complete fossil of these two Cretaceous dinosaurs. The fossil contains the dinosaurs' teeth, skin impressions, and even their stomach contents.

THE UK'S JURASSIC COAST CONTAINS LOTS OF FOSSILS AND STRETCHES FOR 154 KM (96 MILES).

28 PALAEONTOLOGISTS TOOK 28 YEARS TO EXCAVATE AN *ELASMOSAURUS* SKELETON IN THE ANTARCTIC.

Dinosaur world

The giant dinosaurs lived at a time that was very unlike ours. The shape of the continents was different, the climate was warmer, and many of the plants we now take for granted did not exist. It was a another world.

During the Late Jurassic the land was home to a wonderful variety of dinosaurs, ranging from small, agile hunters like *Compsognathus* – here gathered to drink at a lake – to gigantic herbivores like *Brachiosaurus*.

Pangea extended from pole to pole.

Triassic Earth 252–201 MYA
During the Triassic, the first of the three periods that makes up the Mesozoic Era, all the continents that existed before merged into a single landmass known to scientists as Pangea. Much of the land was so far from the ocean that it became desert, but there were lush forests nearer the seashores.

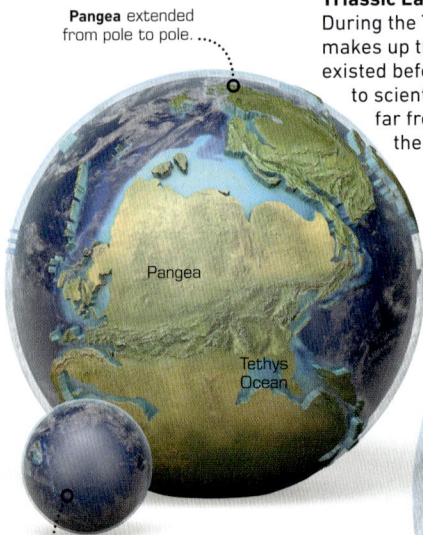

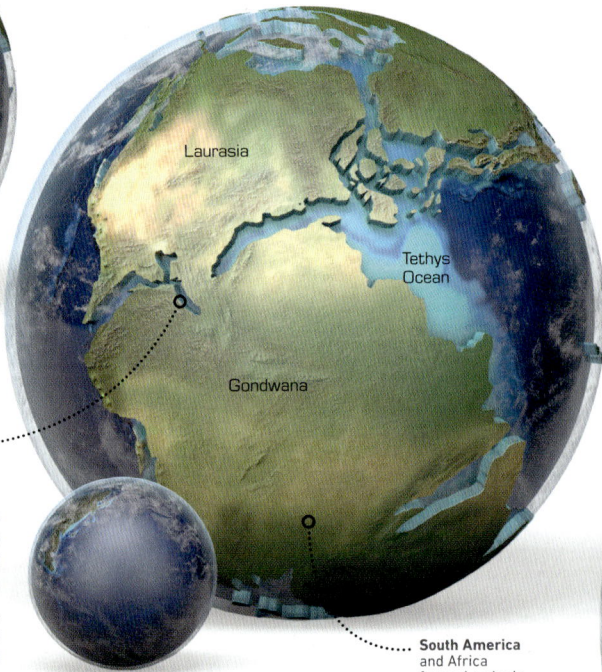

Pangea

Tethys Ocean

Laurasia

Tethys Ocean

Gondwana

Reverse view of the Triassic globe shows the huge ocean.

The link between north and south finally broke about 150 MYA.

Jurassic Earth 201–145 MYA
Pangea was torn apart to form two continents known as Laurasia and Gondwana. The Tethys Ocean that separated them changed the climate, allowing moist air to carry rain over more of the land. As a result, forests spread over regions that had once been deserts.

South America and Africa formed a single landmass.

FAST FACTS

The Atlantic is still expanding from the mid-Atlantic Ridge, forcing North America away from Eurasia at the rate of 2.5 cm (1 in) a year.

North America   Eurasia

Cretaceous means "chalky" because this was the geological period when thick layers of chalk rock began to form at the bottom of tropical seas.

This amazing fossil was discovered in a chalk cliff in Wyoming, USA.

SINCE THERE WAS JUST ONE LANDMASS DURING THE TRIASSIC PERIOD, MOST OF THE ANIMALS WERE VERY SIMILAR.

THE BREAK-UP OF PANGEA ALLOWED DIFFERENT TYPES OF DINOSAUR TO EVOLVE ON SEPARATE CONTINENTS.

HOW DID EARTH CHANGE DURING THE
AGE OF DINOSAURS?

In the Mesozoic Era – the age of giant dinosaurs – the global map was very different from today. Throughout Earth's history the plates that form its rocky crust have been shifting around, carrying the continents with them. By the Triassic Period, this process had pushed them together to form a gigantic supercontinent, surrounded by a vast ocean. But during the rest of the Mesozoic, the landmass began to split up into the continents we know today.

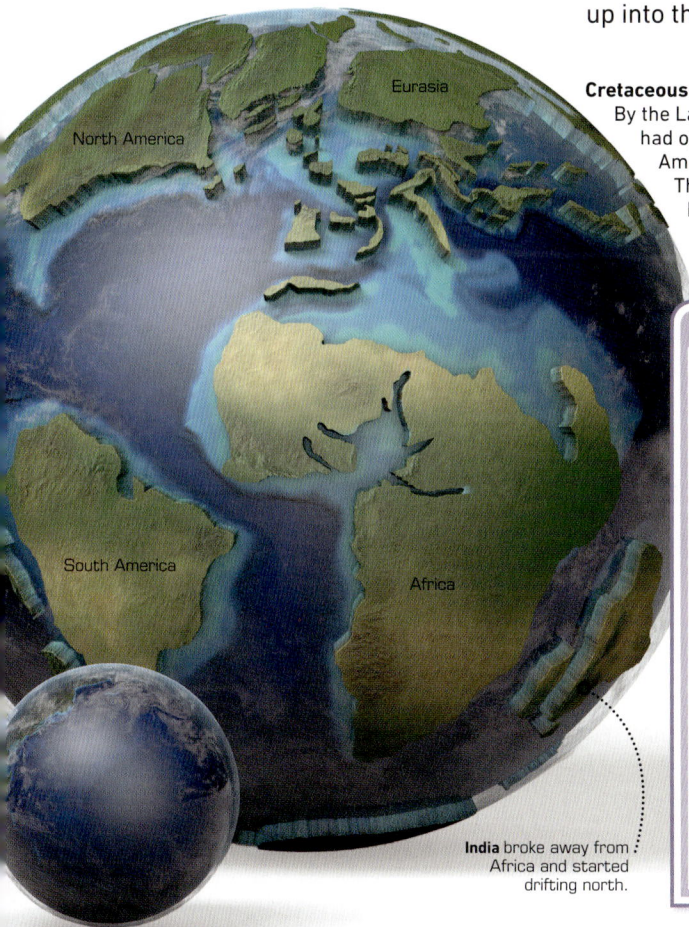

Eurasia

North America

South America

Africa

Cretaceous Earth 145–66 MYA
By the Late Cretaceous, the Atlantic Ocean had opened up, pushing North and South America away from Europe and Africa. The continents we live on today began to take shape, although large areas were underwater.

India broke away from Africa and started drifting north.

CONTINENTAL DRIFT

In 1910, German scientist Alfred Wegener noticed that the eastern coastline of South America could fit into the western coastline of Africa. He proposed that they had once been joined together, but had drifted apart. Nobody believed him, but in the 1960s the new science of plate tectonics proved him right.

The continents fit together like jigsaw pieces.

THE VAST MOUNTAIN RANGES OF THE ROCKIES AND ANDES WERE FORMED DURING THE CRETACEOUS PERIOD.

EVENTUALLY, SOME OF TODAY'S CONTINENTS WILL DRIFT TOGETHER TO FORM NEW SUPERCONTINENTS.

WHAT WAS THE
TRIASSIC
WORLD LIKE?

During the Triassic Period most of the land formed a vast supercontinent with a hostile desert at its heart. The coastal fringes had wetter climates that allowed plants such as mosses, ferns, and conifer trees to grow. But there were no flowering plants, and no buzz of pollinating insects like bees, which had yet to evolve.

Thecodontosaurus
This small plant-eater was one of the earliest dinosaurs. An ancestor of the giant sauropods, it stood on two legs and ran very fast.

Liliensternus
One of the most powerful meat-eating dinosaurs of the Triassic, this agile hunter would have preyed on herbivores like *Plateosaurus*.

Morganucodon
Resembling a modern shrew, and with a similar diet of insects and other small prey, this was one of the earliest mammals.

Diphydontosaurus
At just 10 cm (4 in) long, this tiny reptile was an ancestral relative of the tuatara that still survives in New Zealand.

Plateosaurus
For much of the Triassic the biggest plant-eaters were prosauropods like *Plateosaurus*, which could grow to about 10 m (33 ft) long.

Ferns
Low-growing ferns were vital food for small plant-eaters.

252

TRIASSIC ANIMALS WERE DESCENDED FROM SURVIVORS OF EARTH'S MOST CATASTROPHIC MASS EXTINCTION, WHICH TOOK PLACE 252 MYA.

IT TOOK 10 MILLION YEARS FOR THE **DIVERSITY OF LIFE** TO RECOVER FROM THE MASS EXTINCTION.

Ginkgo
Tall ginkgo trees of
many kinds were
common in Triassic
forests. One species –
Ginkgo biloba – still
exists today.

Eudimorphodon
Unlike the pterosaurs
of later periods,
Eudimorphodon had
a long tail, short neck,
and sharp teeth ideal
for seizing fish.

The animal life of the Triassic was
dominated by reptiles, including some of
the earliest dinosaurs. There were also
various mammal ancestors, which were
soon to become extinct. Small pterosaurs
flew through the air, while even smaller
early mammals scuttled through the
undergrowth in search of insect prey.

Placerias
This hippo-like,
two-tusked animal
was a heavyweight
herbivore related
to the ancestors of
modern mammals.

Titanopteran
With wingspans of up
to 40 cm (16 in), the
titanopterans were
some of the biggest
insects that ever lived.

TURTLES EVOLVED
DURING THE TRIASSIC
AND CONTINUED TO
THRIVE EVEN AFTER
THE DEATH OF THE
DINOSAURS.

During the Jurassic, much of the land was covered with trees, especially conifers, ginkgos, and cycads, but there were still no flowering plants and no grass. In what was to become China, long-necked sauropod dinosaurs browsed in the treetops, stalked by hungry hunters.

Araucarias
These conifer trees – ancestral relatives of the modern monkey puzzle tree – were common during the Jurassic. Some grew to immense heights, putting their tough leaves beyond the reach of even the biggest plant-eating dinosaurs.

Sinraptor
A distant relative of the fearsome *Allosaurus*, this 8-m (26-ft) long hunter prowled the forests of Late Jurassic China in search of prey to ambush and tear apart with its sharp teeth.

Ferns and horsetails
In the absence of grass the ground was carpeted with non-flowering plants, including mosses, ferns, and horsetails.

Docofossor
Like most early mammal-like animals, *Docofossor* was tiny compared to the dinosaurs, at just 9 cm (3.5 in) long. It was specialized for living mainly underground, like a modern mole.

Huayangosaurus
At 4 m (13 ft) long, this was the smallest-known stegosaur – a relative of the much larger *Stegosaurus*, and equipped with a similar array of defensive spikes and plates.

ONE JURASSIC SPECIES OF *ARAUCARIA* COULD GROW TO AN ASTONISHING 100 M (328 FT) – TALLER THAN A 30-STOREY BUILDING.

WHAT WAS THE
JURASSIC WORLD LIKE?

Kunpengopterus
This small pterosaur was able to cling to branches using the fingers and opposable thumb at the bend of each wing. It is the earliest known animal to have such a thumb.

The Triassic ended with a mass extinction that destroyed half of all species, including many big reptiles. But some dinosaurs survived, and their descendants went on to dominate life during the Jurassic Period. Meanwhile, the supercontinent of Pangea split into two landmasses separated by an ocean. This made climates on land wetter and milder, allowing lush ferny forests to flourish. These in turn provided food for the first of the really big plant-eating dinosaurs.

Mamenchisaurus
The incredible neck of *Mamenchisaurus* was up to 12 m (39 ft) long, giving it the ability to reach high into trees to gather leafy food.

Yi qi
Uniquely – as far as we know – this crow-sized feathered dinosaur had wings of stretched skin similar to those of a bat, supported by elongated finger bones.

Sinomacrops
The unusually big eyes of this miniature pterosaur suggest that it probably hunted flying insects at night, like a modern nightjar (a nocturnal bird). It must have been very agile in flight to do this.

Williamsonia
Related to the cycads that thrive today in warm climates, this palm-like plant had a stout woody stem and fern-like leaves. Its foliage was probably eaten by dinosaurs.

SEA LEVELS ROSE DURING THE JURASSIC, FLOODING AREAS THAT ARE NOW DRY LAND, AND CREATING THOUSANDS OF ISLANDS.

WHAT WAS THE
CRETACEOUS
WORLD LIKE?

During the Cretaceous Period, which lasted for 79 million years, the supercontinents of the Jurassic started splitting up. Isolated populations of animals developed in different ways, leading to the evolution of many new types of dinosaur as well as other animals. Meanwhile, flowering plants appeared, along with pollinating insects.

Araucaria
Conifer trees like this *Araucaria* were still common, but new types of tree with flowers and edible fruits were evolving and becoming more dominant.

Edmontosaurus
Equipped with a broad, sharp beak for gathering leaves, this big plant-eating dinosaur had multiple rows of closely packed cheek teeth for grinding the vegetation to an easily digestible pulp.

Hesperornis
This flightless seabird was adapted for hunting underwater, driving itself along with its powerful feet and seizing prey in its toothed bill.

Pteranodon
With a wingspan of up to 6.5 m (21 ft), *Pteranodon* was one of the most spectacular pterosaurs. It probably hunted fish at sea like an albatross.

Mosasaurus
Growing to a colossal 15 m (49 ft) long, *Mosasaurus* was one of the biggest marine reptiles. Its huge jaws made it the deadliest of Late Cretaceous oceanic predators.

MOST OF THE MODERN INSECT GROUPS HAD APPEARED BY THE END OF THE CRETACEOUS, INCLUDING BUTTERFLIES AND GRASSHOPPERS.

Dawn redwood
Related to the giant redwoods of California, USA, this much smaller tree was common during the Cretaceous Period.

Ginkgo
This group of trees evolved 40 million years before the first dinosaurs.

Albertosaurus
A close relative of the larger, more powerful *Tyrannosaurus*, the agile, heavy-jawed *Albertosaurus* prowled the forests and plains of what is now western Canada looking for easy prey.

In North America, the continent was divided by a shallow sea covering what are now the prairies. In the Late Cretaceous, big predators like *Albertosaurus* hunted heavyweight herbivores while spectacular pterosaurs flew over their heads.

Triceratops
Named for its three long horns, which it would have used to defend itself, this elephant-sized herbivore may have been too much to tackle for even a killer like *Albertosaurus*.

Flowering plants
Magnolias were among the first plants to produce flowers. Their showy blooms attracted pollen-feeding insects, which carried some of the pollen to other magnolias.

Bees
The evolution of fragrant, sugary nectar made flowers even more attractive to pollinating insects – especially bees, which evolved from wasps about 130 MYA.

Didelphodon
Similar to a Virginia opossum, this marsupial was one of the largest Cretaceous mammals. It seems to have been a hunter and scavenger, with long, sharp canine teeth and big cheek teeth ideal for crushing small bones.

Struthiomimus
This long-legged, ostrich-like theropod used its toothless beak to gather all kinds of food, and may have foraged on beaches for scraps washed up by the sea.

THE **CLIMATE** DURING THE CRETACEOUS WAS MAINLY WARM – THE AVERAGE GLOBAL TEMPERATURE WAS ABOUT 18°C (64.4°F).

MAGNOLIAS ARE NAMED AFTER THE FRENCH BOTANIST PIERRE MAGNOL.

WHAT HAPPENED TO THE
DINOSAURS?

The Mesozoic age of giant dinosaurs ended 66 MYA, in a
mass extinction that killed off all the giants as well as
many other animals. The date coincides with the impact
of a colossal meteorite – probably an asteroid – that hit
Mexico and caused a gigantic explosion. The event would
have killed everything over a vast area instantly, and had
catastrophic consequences for all life on Earth.

DISCOVERY

All over the world, a thin layer
of clay forms a 66-million-year-old
line in the rocks. The significance
of this was not understood until
1980, when American scientist
Luis Alvarez and his son Walter
discovered that the clay is rich in
iridium, a metal rare on Earth but
common in meteorites. They
proposed that the clay was fall-out
from the impact of a colossal space
rock — and that this was the event
that destroyed the giant dinosaurs.

Iridium
layer

The asteroid that slammed into Earth was at least
10 km (6 miles) across – the width of the US city
of San Francisco – and travelling at an estimated
130,000 kph (80,000 mph). When it was stopped dead
by the impact, all the energy of its speed was instantly
turned into heat. This vaporized the asteroid in an
explosion that was some 2 million times
more powerful than the biggest
nuclear bomb ever
detonated.

HUGE **VOLCANIC
ERUPTIONS** IN
INDIA ALSO HELPED
CAUSE THE MASS
EXTINCTION.

WITH FEWER **PLANTS**
AFTER THE ASTEROID
IMPACT, BIG HERBIVORES
STARVED TO DEATH.
THIS MEANT LESS FOOD
FOR BIG CARNIVORES.

Made of solid rock, the killer asteroid was the size and weight of Mount Everest.

Scientists estimate that **75% of animal life** was wiped out within hours of the impact.

LIFE ON EARTH TOOK MILLIONS OF YEARS TO RECOVER FROM THE EFFECTS OF THE **ASTEROID IMPACT**.

DROPLETS OF MOLTEN ROCK CREATED BY THE EXPLOSION, CALLED **SPHERULES**, ARE FOUND THROUGHOUT THE WORLD.

IMPACT!

The huge asteroid that ended the reign of the giant dinosaurs crashed into the sea near the north coast of Mexico's Yucatán Peninsula. The explosion on impact destroyed all life in the region, and the shock wave generated huge oceanic tsunamis that swept around the globe, flooding coastal areas. Trillions of tons of dust and water vapour were hurled into the atmosphere, blocking out sunlight and causing global climate change. The impact left a crater 180 km (112 miles) wide, now buried more than 1 km (0.6 miles) below the ground.

Molten rock blown into the air by the explosion triggered wildfires across the globe.

FAST FACTS

Marsupials — the pouched mammals — suffered badly during the extinction, especially in North America and Eurasia. But they survived in South America, and in Australia they went on to dominate the native wildlife.

Koala

The pterosaurs had evolved into the most spectacular flying animals that ever existed, but the extinction sealed their fate and they vanished off the face of the Earth.

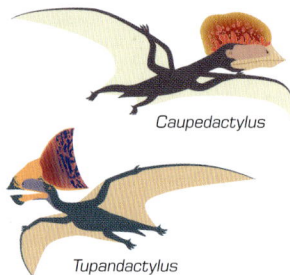

Caupedactylus

Tupandactylus

This South American rhea is similar to many extinct theropod dinosaurs, but its ancestors managed to escape their fate.

The largest mammals to get through the disaster were no bigger than this American badger.

Insects such as this dragonfly may have survived because they were small and mobile.

Invertebrates
Many types of marine invertebrate died out, including the ammonites. Land invertebrates such as insects were also hard hit, but enough survived to re-populate the planet.

Mammals
Nearly all the mammals alive before the catastrophe were small, mainly burrowing animals. Their underground homes may have given them some protection, since many types of mammal survived.

Birds
Most groups of bird were killed off, but relatives of ostriches survived, as did the ancestors of seabirds, songbirds, and birds of prey, among others. They are all living dinosaurs.

THE DIVERSITY OF BIRDS MAKES DINOSAURS SOME OF THE MOST SUCCESSFUL ANIMALS THAT HAVE EVER LIVED.

ALTHOUGH SOME GIANT LAND MAMMALS EVOLVED AFTER THE EXTINCTION, NONE WERE AS BIG AS THE LARGEST DINOSAURS.

WHICH ANIMALS ESCAPED
EXTINCTION?

The catastrophe that destroyed the giant dinosaurs had a disastrous impact on all life on Earth. But some types of animal – including a few feathered dinosaurs – avoided extinction. Quite how they managed this is not known, and they probably only survived in small numbers. Gradually, the world recovered, food became easier to find, and over many millions of years their descendants evolved into the animals that live around us today.

GIANT MAMMALS

After the extinction, much bigger mammals started evolving to take the place of giant dinosaurs. Eventually, this led to the appearance of "megaherbivores" such as the rhino-like *Uintatherium*, which grew to 4 m (13 ft) long.

Uintatherium

The origins of the three main groups of living frog can be traced back to just after the extinction.

The tuatara of New Zealand is a survivor from the age of dinosaurs.

Living underwater may have helped many fish avoid extinction.

Amphibians
Some forms of amphibian were destroyed by the extinction event, but those that escaped thrived in the new era. Frogs, in particular, enjoyed a dramatic increase in diversity.

Reptiles
Many groups of reptiles fared better than their dinosaur relatives. They included turtles, lizards, snakes, and crocodiles. But the airborne pterosaurs and many marine reptiles disappeared.

Fish
Sharks and rays were quite badly hit, with many groups becoming extinct. But most families of bony fish – the more familiar ray-finned, scaly types like this perch – survived and thrived.

MANY MAMMALS SURVIVED THE CATASTROPHE, BUT A QUARTER OF ALL LIVING MAMMAL SPECIES ARE NOW UNDER THREAT.

WE ARE LIVING AT THE BEGINNING OF ANOTHER MASS EXTINCTION – BUT THIS ONE HAS BEEN CAUSED BY HUMAN ACTIVITY.

LATE BIRDS

The birds that survived the extinction 66 MYA were probably quite small, but some of their descendants evolved into giants. They included a massively built flightless bird called *Gastornis* that prowled the forests of North America and Europe about 50 MYA. Up to 2 m (6.5 ft) tall, it had an immensely strong bill that it may have used to break into tough-shelled nuts lying on the forest floor, seize and kill other animals, or even crack the bones of the dead.

With its stout legs and feet, *Gastornis* looked very like its dinosaur ancestors.

Euoplocephalus
Canada
This big plant-eating dinosaur lived about 75 MYA. It was covered with bony armour for defence against hungry tyrannosaurs, and could fight back with its heavy tail club.

Issi
Greenland
In the Triassic, the land that became Greenland was home to this prosauropod – a type of long-necked plant-eater that was an ancestor of the biggest dinosaurs of all.

Pachycephalosaurus
Canada and USA
The biggest of the dome-headed dinosaurs lived some 70 MYA. Its skull was 30 cm (12 in) thick, and probably adapted for sidelong head-butting battles with rival males.

Liopleurodon
Germany
This marine reptile was one of the most fearsome hunters in Jurassic seas. It had huge jaws, which it used to seize other marine reptiles and rip them apart – although it could swallow the smaller ones whole.

Dreadnoughtus
Argentina
Thought to be one of the largest dinosaurs to have walked the planet, this giant sauropod grew to 26 m (85 ft) long and weighed a colossal 59 tonnes (65 tons).

Cryolophosaurus
Antarctica
The fossil remains of this big hunter were found in 1991, showing that Antarctica was once a thriving wildlife habitat. It had a unique bony crest on its head, which may have been used to attract mates. *Cryolophosaurus* was one of the biggest predators on Earth.

Heterodontosaurus
Africa
This plant-eater lived in the Jurassic Period, about 200 MYA. It was no bigger than a turkey and had unusual dagger-like canine teeth, which were probably used for defence, display, and even fighting rivals.

40 CANADA'S **DINOSAUR PROVINCIAL PARK** HAS THE MOST DINOSAUR TYPES FOUND AT A SINGLE SITE, WITH 40 SPECIES.

NOT MANY **FOSSILS** HAVE BEEN FOUND IN AUSTRALIA AND NEW ZEALAND – MUCH OF THE LAND WAS COVERED BY SEA DURING THE MESOZOIC ERA.

WHERE HAVE FOSSILS
BEEN FOUND?

Fossils occur worldwide, but they are usually found on coasts and in open landscapes where sedimentary rocks formed from beds of mud and clay are exposed to the air. The fossils are revealed as the rocks crumble, and scientists can then dig them out. But there are many fossils still to be found in regions covered by dense forests or even ice.

Woolly mammoth
Siberia
During the most recent ice age, the grassy northern fringes of Asia were the habitat of the woolly mammoth. Some mammoths fell into swamps that then froze, preserving their bodies almost intact.

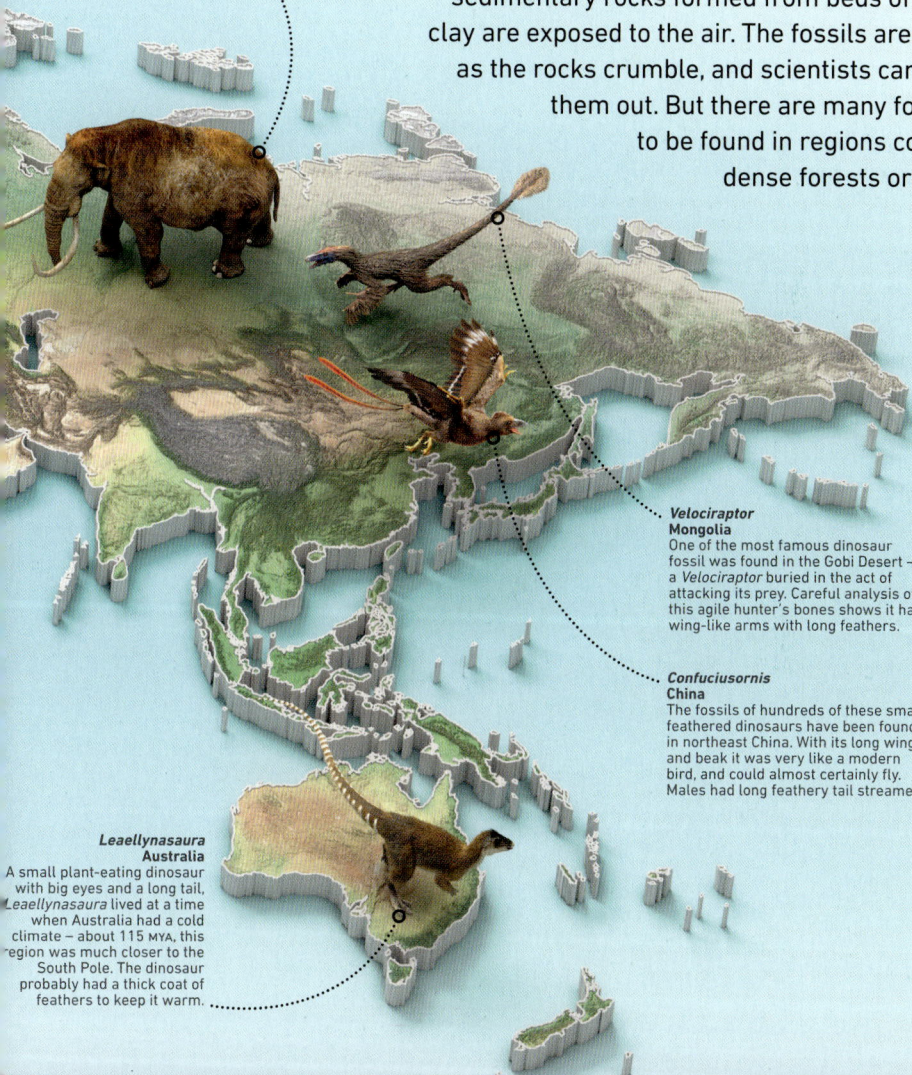

Velociraptor
Mongolia
One of the most famous dinosaur fossil was found in the Gobi Desert – a *Velociraptor* buried in the act of attacking its prey. Careful analysis of this agile hunter's bones shows it had wing-like arms with long feathers.

Confuciusornis
China
The fossils of hundreds of these small feathered dinosaurs have been found in northeast China. With its long wings and beak it was very like a modern bird, and could almost certainly fly. Males had long feathery tail streamers.

Leaellynasaura
Australia
A small plant-eating dinosaur with big eyes and a long tail, *Leaellynasaura* lived at a time when Australia had a cold climate – about 115 MYA, this region was much closer to the South Pole. The dinosaur probably had a thick coat of feathers to keep it warm.

THE YOUNGEST PERSON TO FIND A DINOSAUR FOSSIL WAS 3-YEAR-OLD DAVID SHIFFLER, WHO FOUND A DINOSAUR EGG FRAGMENT IN THE USA.

FISH FOSSILS HAVE BEEN FOUND NEAR THE SUMMIT OF MOUNT EVEREST, PROVING THAT ITS ROCKS WERE FORMED BENEATH AN OCEAN.

Dinosaur science

LOOKING MUCH CLOSER

Scientists have made new discoveries about dinosaurs by using modern technology to re-examine the fossils in museum collections.

Inside view

The complex X-ray technology of medical **CT scanners** enables scientists to probe inside fossils without destroying them. This revealed large air-filled cavities in the skull of **Majungasaurus**, a powerful predator that lived from 70 to 66 MYA.

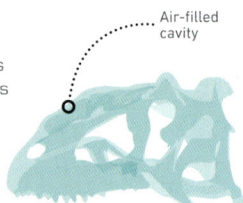

Air-filled cavity

Microfossils

By using a scanning **electron microscope**, a scientist can examine fossils at astonishingly high magnifications, revealing details of their cell structure. This has been used to identify colour cells in the plumage of feathered dinosaurs, giving clues to their colour when alive.

Male or female?

In 2005, chemical analysis of a fossil **Tyrannosaurus** leg bone showed that it contained medullary bone — a type of calcium-rich tissue found in female birds that helps them form their eggs. This proved beyond doubt that the dinosaur was a female.

HOW MEGALOSAURUS HAS CHANGED

Over the two centuries since the first known dinosaur was named in 1824, our ideas about what *Megalosaurus* looked like have changed dramatically.

1850s

A model of **Megalosaurus** was unveiled at Crystal Palace Park in the UK in 1851. It shows us how the scientists of the time reconstructed it as resembling a lizard.

1970s

The discovery of large theropod hunters like **Allosaurus** that stood on two legs made scientists rethink Megalosaurus. They realized that Megalosaurus would have looked similar.

2020s

Modern techniques for reconstructing extinct dinosaurs have made it clear that Megalosaurus was an **agile predator** that ran with its head and body balanced by a heavy tail.

A 2018 STUDY OF THE EGGS OF *DEINONYCHUS* – A CLOSE RELATIVE OF *VELOCIRAPTOR* – SHOW THEY WERE BLUE WITH BROWN SPECKLES.

SCIENTISTS HAVE MANAGED TO RECOVER *SOFT TISSUE* FROM 68-MILLION-YEAR-OLD DINOSAUR BONES BY DISSOLVING THEM IN ACID.

CLUES TO THE
PAST

By studying the anatomy and behaviour of **living animals**, we can learn a lot about how dinosaurs may have lived in the distant past.

Showing off

Rival **red deer stags** may lock antlers in combat, but mostly they use them to show off. **Horned dinosaurs** may have done the same — the animal with the biggest horns being top of the pecking order.

Eggs in nests

A **mother hen** incubates her eggs and protects her chicks by covering them with her feathery wings. A fossil of the 80-million-year-old theropod dinosaur **Citipati** shows that it did exactly the same.

BACK TO LIFE

The technologies of **computer science** and robotics are giving scientists new insights into how these spectacular animals functioned when alive.

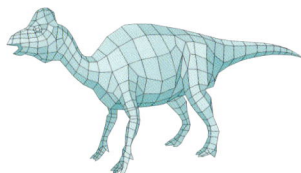

Computer modelling

Using evidence gathered from fossils, scientists can build **computer models** showing how the muscles and bones of dinosaurs worked together. The models can be animated so they **walk, run, and even bite**.

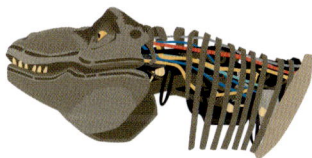

Robotic replicas

Engineers can make **robotic replicas** of dinosaurs to test the ideas explored by computer modelling. This mechanical **Tyrannosaurus** has been used to see if it really could bite with the force needed to crush bone.

LAST DAYS OF THE
GIANTS

Experts agree that the giant dinosaurs were wiped out by an asteroid strike 66 MYA. A recently discovered fossil site known as Tanis in North Dakota, USA, preserves the remains of animals killed on the day of the impact 3,000 km (1,900 miles) away. They include fish with gills clogged by debris from the explosion and dinosaur bodies torn apart by the cataclysmic shock wave.

UNTIL THE TECHNIQUE OF USING RADIOACTIVITY TO DATE ROCKS WAS INVENTED IN 1907, WE HAD NO WAY OF KNOWING THE TRUE AGE OF FOSSILS.

THE FOSSIL SITE TANIS IS NAMED AFTER AN ANCIENT EGYPTIAN CITY THAT WAS FOUNDED AT LEAST 3,000 YEARS AGO.

GLOSSARY

AMBER
Sticky resin that has oozed from a tree and become hardened over many millions of years.

AMPHIBIAN
A vertebrate animal that usually starts life in water as a tadpole. It turns into an air-breathing adult, such as a frog, that lives partly on land.

ANCESTOR
An animal or plant species from which a more recent species has evolved.

ANKYLOSAUR
One of the main types of ornithischian dinosaur, with a body that was covered with bony armour.

AQUATIC
Describes something that lives in water.

ARCHOSAUR
One of a group of animals that includes, or included, the dinosaurs, birds, pterosaurs, and crocodiles.

ARID
Describes a very dry climate or place.

ARTHROPODS
Invertebrates with segmented bodies and a hard outer covering (exoskeleton). Extinct arthropods include trilobites and eurypterids. Living ones include insects and spiders.

ASTEROID
A large rocky object in orbit around the Sun – bigger than a meteor but smaller than a planet.

BINOCULAR VISION
Seeing a scene or object with two eyes, so an animal can see in depth, or 3-D.

BREEDING
Males and females coming together to produce eggs and/or young.

CAMBRIAN
A period of the Paleozoic Era, lasting from 541 to 485 MYA.

CAMOUFLAGE
Colours and patterns that make an animal hard to see.

CARBONIFEROUS
A period of the Paleozoic Era that lasted from 359 to 298 MYA.

CARRION
The remains of dead animals that other animals eat.

CONIFER
A plant – usually a tall tree such as a pine or spruce – that carries its seeds in scaly cones.

CONTINENT
A big landmass that is made of rocks that are different from the rocks of the ocean floors.

CONTINENTAL DRIFT
The movement of continents across the surface of the Earth over time.

COPROLITES
Fossilized animal droppings, which often contain fragments of the animal's food.

CRETACEOUS
The third period of the Mesozoic Era (the age of dinosaurs), which began 145 MYA and ended 66 MYA.

CYANOBACTERIA
Bacteria that can use sunlight to manufacture their own food by photosynthesis.

CYCAD
A tropical plant that bears its seeds in large cones, but has a crown of foliage, like a tree fern or palm.

DNA
Short for deoxyribonucleic acid, a very long molecule made up of small individual units. DNA is found in the cells of all living things; the order of the small units "spells out" the genetic instructions (genes) of the individual.

EMBRYO
A plant, animal, or other organism in an early stage of development from an egg or a seed.

EQUATOR
An imaginary line drawn around Earth that is equally distant from both the North and South Pole.

ERA
A span of geological time that defines a phase of the history of life, such as the Paleozoic or Mesozoic.

EXOSKELETON
An external skeleton. Animals such as crabs have an exoskeleton. In contrast, humans have an internal skeleton.

FERN
A primitive type of non-flowering plant with leafy fronds that grows in damp places, and has tall stems.

FLIPPERS
Limbs with broad paddle blades adapted for efficient swimming.

FOOD CHAIN
A linked series of livings things (animals and plants), each of which is the food for the next in line.

FOSSIL
The remains or traces of any living thing that survive the normal processes of decay, and are often preserved by being turned to stone.

FOSSILIZATION
The process by which the remains of living things turn into fossils.

GINKGO
One of a group of non-flowering plants that grows into a tall tree with more or less triangular leaves.

GONDWANA
The southern supercontinent made up of Africa, Australia, Antarctica, South America, and India.

HORSETAIL
A primitive type of plant that produces spores instead of seeds, and has thread-like leaves that grow from the stem in rings.

ICE AGE
A period of time during which global temperatures fall and sheets of ice (glaciers) cover large areas of land.

ICHTHYOSAUR
One of a group of dolphin-like marine reptiles that was very common in the early Mesozoic Era.

INVERTEBRATE
An animal without a vertebral column (backbone).

JURASSIC
The second of three periods making up the Mesozoic Era, from 201 to 145 MYA.

KERATIN
A tough structural protein found in hair, feathers, scales, claws, and horns.

LAURASIA
The northern supercontinent made up of North America, Europe, and Asia.

LIMESTONE
A rock made of calcite (lime), and often built up from the skeletons of microscopic marine life.

MAMMAL
One of a group of warm-blooded, often hairy vertebrates that feed their young on milk supplied by the mother.

MAMMOTH
A type of elephant with long tusks that lived during the Pliocene and Pleistocene. During the last ice age, some mammoths developed long hair, which helped them stay warm.

MANIRAPTORAN
An advanced type of theropod dinosaur with powerful arms and claws, which gave rise to the birds. Maniraptoran means "hand-grabber".

MARINE REPTILE
A reptile that lives in the sea, but also the plesiosaurs, ichthyosaurs, and similar groups that became extinct at the end of the Mesozoic Era.

MARSUPIAL
A mammal such as a kangaroo that gives birth to very small live young and rears them in a pouch.

MASS EXTINCTION
A disaster that causes the disappearance of many types of life.

MEGAHERBIVORE
A very large plant-eating animal.

MESOZOIC
The era known as the age of dinosaurs, from 252 to 66 MYA.

MICROFOSSIL
A fossil that is too small to be studied without using a microscope. It may be a fossil of a microscopic form of life, or part of a larger form of life.

MOSASAUR
A giant, sea-dwelling lizard that lived during the Cretaceous Period. It was a fierce predator with a slender body, long snout, and flipper-like limbs.

MOSS
A primitive type of non-flowering plant that forms cushion-like growths in damp places.

MYA
Million Years Ago.

NECTAR
A sugary fluid produced by flowers to attract insects and other animals.

NEOGENE
The second period of the Cenozoic Era, lasting from 23 to 2 MYA.

NUTRIENTS
Substances that living things need to build their tissues.

ORNITHOPOD
One of a group of plant-eating dinosaurs that mostly walked on their hind legs and were not armoured.

OSTEODERMS
Bony plates that form within the skin and often form the basis of defensive armour.

PALAEONTOLOGIST
A scientist who studies fossilized finds, including animals and plants.

PERIOD
A span of geological time that is part of an era – for example, the Jurassic Period is part of the Mesozoic Era.

PETRIFICATION
A form of fossilization where the detailed structures of an original organism are replaced by minerals, sometimes in a way that preserves very fine details.

PLESIOSAUR
A marine reptile with four long flippers; many had very long necks.

PLIOSAUR
A type of plesiosaur, with a shorter neck, larger head and jaws, and a more predatory lifestyle.

POLLINATING
Carrying pollen from one plant to another, as bees do.

PREDATOR
An animal that kills other animals for food.

PREY
An animal that is killed and eaten by another animal.

PROSAUROPOD
One of a group of early long-necked, plant-eating dinosaurs, which lived in the Triassic and Jurassic before the sauropods.

PROTOFEATHERS
Hair-like structures that provided insulation and later evolved into feathers.

PTEROSAUR
One of the flying reptiles that lived during the Mesozoic Era, with wings of stretched skin that were supported by the bones of a single elongated finger.

REPTILE
One of the group of animals that includes crocodiles, snakes, pterosaurs, turtles, lizards, and dinosaurs.

SAUROPOD
One of the group of long-necked, plant-eating dinosaurs that evolved from the prosauropods.

SCAVENGER
An animal that lives on the remains of dead animals and other scraps.

SEDIMENT
Solid particles, such as sand, silt, or mud, that have settled in layers.

SEDIMENTARY ROCKS
Rocks made of hardened sediments.

SERRATED
Saw-toothed, like a bread knife.

SPECIES
A particular type of living thing that can breed with others of the same type.

SPONGES
A large group (phylum) of marine invertebrates with a very simple structure that feed by creating currents through their bodies and filtering small particles from the water. They have no muscles or nerve cells. Many have skeletons built of small hard elements called spicules.

STEGOSAUR
One of a group of armoured dinosaurs with large plates and spines on their backs.

STROMATOLITES
These structures were created in shallow, warm water by sheets of blue-green algae and trapped sediments. Fossil stromatolites are evidence of early life.

SUPERCONTINENT
A huge landmass made up of many continents that have joined together.

TETHYS OCEAN
A tropical ocean that separated Gondwana and Laurasia. It was eventually closed by the northward movement of Africa and India.

TETRAPOD
A vertebrate with four limbs (arms, legs, or wings). All amphibians, reptiles, mammals, and birds are tetrapods. Snakes are also tetrapods because they evolved from ancestors with four limbs.

THEROPOD
One of the group of saurischian dinosaurs that are nearly all meat-eaters.

TITANOSAUR
One of a group of sauropods that evolved in the Cretaceous Period.

TRACE FOSSIL
A fossil that preserves the activity of a living thing, rather than the living thing itself – for example, a dinosaur footprint.

TRACKWAY
A trail of fossilized dinosaur footprints.

TRIASSIC
The first period of the Mesozoic Era, from 252 to 201 MYA.

TUNDRA
A treeless region dominated by low-growing, cold-tolerant plants.

VERTEBRAE
The bones that make up the backbone of an animal such as a dinosaur, bird, or mammal.

VERTEBRATE
An animal with an internal skeleton and backbone.

WARM-BLOODED
Animals that maintain a constant internal body temperature are described as warm-blooded. Mammals and birds are warm-blooded, whereas fish and reptiles are cold-blooded.

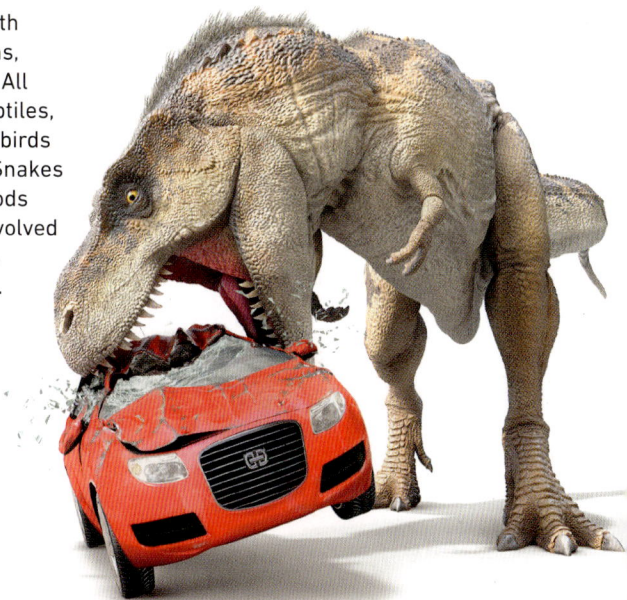

INDEX

ACKNOWLEDGMENTS

The publisher would like to thank the following people for their help with making the book: Chris Barker for additional text, Scarlett O'Hara for proofreading, and Helen Peters for the index.

The publisher would like to thank the following for permission to reproduce their images:

(Key: a-above; b-below/bottom; c-centre; f-far; l-left; r-right; t-top)

1 Dreamstime.com: Jana Kopilova (texture). 2 TurboSquid: 3d_wanderer (tr). 3 TurboSquid: BenJewer (b). 4 Science Photo Library: James Kuether (tc); Mark Williamson (tr). 5 Alamy Stock Photo: Dotted Zebra (tr). Dreamstime.com: Planetfelicity (cl). 6-7 Science Photo Library: James Kuether. 8 Alamy Stock Photo: Florilegius (tr). 9 TurboSquid: Vladislav Egorov (cb). 12-13 Alamy Stock Photo: Dotted Zebra. 15 TurboSquid: Shao 999D (bl). 16-17 Alamy Stock Photo: Mohamad Haghani. 21 Alamy Stock Photo: dpa picture alliance (crb). 23 TurboSquid: 3d_wanderer (cr). 24-25 Science Photo Library: Dirk Wiersma. 26 Velizar A. Simeonovski: Caihong juji. Velizar Simeonovski after the direction of Julia Clarke and Chad Eliason (t). 28 Dorling Kindersley: Andy Crawford / Robert L. Braun - modelmaker (cla). 29 Alamy Stock Photo: Martin Shields (cra). TurboSquid: coolnidz (cla). 31 Getty Images: Dwi Yulianto / EyeEm (crb). 32-33 Getty Images / iStock: Warpaintcobra. 34 Shutterstock.com: Albert Beukhof (clb); PJ photography (cl). 38-39 Science Photo Library: Mark Williamson. 47 TurboSquid: BenJewer. 49 R. McKellar (Royal SK Museum): (cla). 50-51 Alamy

Stock Photo: PA Images / Jonathan Brady. 54 Dreamstime.com: Linda Bucklin (cl). 54-55 Dreamstime.com: Robyn Mackenzie. 55 Dorling Kindersley: James Kuether (crb). 56 Alamy Stock Photo: Kevin Schafer (clb). Dreamstime.com: Vladislav Gajic / Vladislav (cl). 56-57 Dreamstime.com: Judith Kiener (dentures); Saskia Massink. 57 Alamy Stock Photo: Natural History Museum, London (cra). 59 Alamy Stock Photo: Natural History Museum, London (clb). 60-61 Science Photo Library: Jose Antonio Peas. 62 Science Photo Library: Julius T Csotonyi (clb). 62-63 Science Photo Library: Jaime Chirinos. 63 Dorling Kindersley: Peter Minister / Peter Minister, Digital Sculptor (ca). Getty Images: Antic Andrej / EyeEm (tr). 64-65 Dorling Kindersley: Jon Hughes (c). 64 Alamy Stock Photo: Life on white (cb). 66-67 Science Photo Library: James Kuether. 69 Alamy Stock Photo: Thiriet / Andia (tc). Shutterstock.com: ChameleonsEye (tr). 71 Dorling Kindersley: Andy Crawford Courtesy of Dorset Dinosaur Museum (cr). Science Photo Library: Jaime Chirinos (cb). 74-75 Getty Images / iStock: cynoclub (cb). 74 Dreamstime.com: Yobro10 (cb). Science Photo Library: Sebastian Kaulitzki (crb). 75 123RF.com: Chainarong (cra). 77 E. Ray Garton, Curator, Prehistoric Planet: (cl). 78 E. Ray Garton, Curator, Prehistoric Planet: 79 123RF.com: Corey A Ford (cla). Dorling Kindersley: Tracy Morgan; R.A. Strudwick; C.Carter (clb). 80-81 Science Photo Library: Mark Garlick. 83 Alamy Stock Photo: Richard Becker (tc). Dreamstime.com: John A. Anderson (tr); Yunona Shimanskaya (tl). 86-87 Dreamstime.com: Planetfelicity.

88 Getty Images / iStock: dottedhippo (clb). 90-91 Alamy Stock Photo: Album. 92 Alamy Stock Photo: Corbin17 (clb). 94 Alamy Stock Photo: Sergey Krasovskiy / Stocktrek Images (cb). Dorling Kindersley: Colin Keates / Natural History Museum, London (bc). 95 Alamy Stock Photo: Giedrius Stakauskas (crb). Getty Images: Gallo Images ROOTS RF collection / Daryl Balfour (crb/Ostrich). Science Photo Library: Jaime Chirinos (cra). 96-97 Science Photo Library: Jaime Chirinos. 99 Dreamstime.com: Hongqi Zhang (aka Michael Zhang) (crb). TurboSquid: all15USD (c). 100-101 Alamy Stock Photo: blickwinkel / McPHOTO / MKD. 103 Alamy Stock Photo: Natural History Museum, London (cra). 104 Alamy Stock Photo: Dotted Zebra (clb). 105 123RF.com: Michael Rosskothen (cra). 106-107 Alamy Stock Photo: Natural History Museum, London. 111 TurboSquid: Dibia Digital. 112-113 Science Photo Library: Jaime Chirinos. 114-115 Getty Images / iStock: IgorKovalchuk (c). 115 Alamy Stock Photo: All Canada Photos / Wayne Lynch (cra). Dorling Kindersley: Harry Taylor / Natural History Museum, London (cr). Getty Images / iStock: geckophoto (c). 116-117 Science Photo Library: Roman Uchytel. 118 Science Photo Library: Roman Uchytel (clb). 119 Dorling Kindersley: Andrew Nelmerm / Royal British Columbia Museum, Victoria, Canada (c). 125 Alamy Stock Photo: William Mullins (cla). Dorling Kindersley: James Kuether (ca) Getty Images: The Image Bank Unreleased / Naturfoto Honal (c). 127 Alamy Stock Photo: Cultura Creative RF / Gregory S. Paulson (cra). 128-129 Depositphotos Inc: NDerkach. 130-131 123RF.com: Athikhun Boonrin (c). Alamy Stock Photo: Xavier Fores - Joana Roncero (t).

Dreamstime.com: Leigh Prather (c). 130 Dorling Kindersley: Colin Keates / Natural History Museum (clb). 131 Alamy Stock Photo: Kitti Kahotong (cr); wonderlandstock (clb). Science Photo Library: Patrick Dumas / Look At Sciences (tr). Shutterstock.com: Suwat wongkham (crb). 132-133 Alamy Stock Photo: Phil Degginger. 134 Shutterstock.com: Alex Coan (cla) 135 Alamy Stock Photo: Nobumichi Tamura / Stocktrek Images (cra). 136 Alamy Stock Photo: Oleksandr Kharchenko (cl). 138 Alamy Stock Photo: Jill Stephenson (cla). 140 Alamy Stock Photo: Nobumichi Tamura / Stocktrek Images (tr). 140-141 Science Photo Library: Mark Garlick. 141 Dorling Kindersley: James Kuether (crb). 142-143 Alamy Stock Photo: aroundtheworld.photography (c). 146-147 Alamy Stock Photo: Dotted Zebra. 148-149 Dorling Kindersley: Simon Mumford / Colorado Plateau Geosystems Inc (c). 148 Dorling Kindersley: Simon Mumford / Colorado Plateau Geosystems Inc (t). Science Photo Library: Dirk Wiersma (crb). 156-157 TurboSquid: BlueModels. 156 Alamy Stock Photo: Rosanne Tackaberry (clb). 157 TurboSquid: corsican (t). 158-159 Science Photo Library: Detlev Van Ravenswaay. 160 Alamy Stock Photo: Ger Bosma (cr). Dreamstime.com: Lucielang (tc). Shutterstock.com: Arizona Daily Pics (c). 161 123RF.com: Eric Isselee (clb). Dreamstime.com: Sneekerp (crb). Getty Images / iStock: cynoclub (crb/aquarium). 162-163 Science Photo Library: Jaime Chirinos. 164 TurboSquid: (cb). 165 TurboSquid: DisneyTD (cla)

All other images
© Dorling Kindersley

For further information see:
www.dkimages.com